Helping Your Teenager Beat Depressio

A Problem-Solving
Approach for Families

Katharina Manassis, MD, FRCPC
Anne Marie Levac, RN, MN

Woodbine House • 2004

All rights reserved under International and Pan-American copyright laws. Published in the United States of America by Woodbine House, Inc., 6510 Bells Mill Road, Bethesda, MD 20817. 800-843-7323. www.woodbinehouse.com

Publisher's note: *The information contained in this book is not intended as a substitute for consultation with your child's healthcare providers. Although the authors, editor, and publisher made every attempt to ensure that the information in this book was up to date and accurate at the time of publication, recommended treatments and drug therapies may change as new medical or scientific information becomes available. Additionally, the authors, editor, and publisher are not responsible for errors or omissions or for consequences from application of this book. Any practice described in this book should be applied by the reader in close consultation with a qualified physician.*

Library of Congress Cataloging-in-Publication Data

Manassis, Katharina.
  Helping your teenager beat depression : a problem-solving approach for families / Katharina Manassis, Anne Marie Levac.
     p. cm.
  Includes bibliographical references and index.
  ISBN 1-890627-49-6 (trade pbk.)
 1. Depression in adolescence—Popular works. 2. Cognitive therapy—Popular works. 3. Parent and child—Popular works. I. Levac, Anne Marie. II. Title.
  RJ506.D4M265 2004
  616.85'2700835—dc22

                                                                    2004006762

Manufactured in the United States of America

First edition

10 9 8 7 6 5 4 3 2 1

Dedication

Dedicated to adolescents
and their families who experience depression.
May this book provide support, hope, and
some good practical advice.

Acknowledgements

●

We wish to acknowledge the generous support
of the Tremain family, which allowed us
to pursue the research on which
this program is based.

The authors and publisher also wish to thank
Charles B. Whitehead, Psy.D. for his
review of the manuscript.

Table of Contents

Introduction

Kayla: *Kayla was a sixteen-year-old girl who lived with her mother, stepfather, older sister, and younger half brother. Kayla's parents had divorced five years ago. Her mother and stepfather had been married for three years, and Kayla had never really adjusted well to the new family structure. She got along with her stepfather and connected with him around some interests such as horses and hiking. She saw her father every other weekend but did not feel particularly close to him. Overall, she felt increasingly isolated from her family, reporting that no one really understood her. Kayla became more pensive, withdrawn, and lethargic and spent hours in her room. She continued to manage well at school and would talk to friends when they called, but rarely initiated the contacts. She often declined invitations to parties or dances, stating that she was too tired or simply not interested.*

Mark: *Mark was a twelve-year-old boy who lived with his parents and younger sister. According to his parents, Mark had enjoyed school until about two years ago, when he started complaining about other kids teasing him and not wanting to be his friend, as well as finding the school work too hard. His parents met with teachers, who reported that Mark was academically strong although not applying himself. He tended to isolate himself from his peers and often made negative comments to others. In the past three months, his parents had noticed he was more irritable with his sister, negative about himself, and often refused to join the family on outings.*

Mark frequently complained about various aches and pains, particularly on Sunday nights. Getting ready for school on Monday mornings became more and more challenging, and he told his parents he hated school.

Janice: Janice was a fourteen-year-old girl who lived with her mother in a single parent family. Her parents had separated several years previously, and she had no contact with her father. He drank excessively and had been abusive to her mother. Janice was generally a very good student in her first year of high school, and was active in baseball and karate.

Janice stopped attending her church youth group two months before being referred for a mental health assessment. Her marks at mid-term were close to failing, and she was skipping afternoon classes to come home while her mother was at work. She was tired and had lost weight. She spent her afternoons repeatedly phoning her mother at work. At night, she couldn't get to sleep, and woke up within a few hours when she did. She denied ever being successful at anything, didn't think she could ever be successful at anything, and described herself as a "loser." Her mother brought her to the assessment because she was concerned Janice might be depressed.

How This Book Can Help You and Your Teen

Mark, Janice, and Kayla represent three of the many faces of teenage depression. Perhaps your teen sounds similar to one of these teens in particular, or he may share some characteristics of two or more of these teens. If your teen is as troubled by depression as Janice is, look for more immediate help. Teens with this type of depression need psychotherapy, medication, or both to recover. Parents can help with that recovery, but a mental health professional is also clearly needed.

If your teen resembles Mark or Kayla, the book may be used on its own for a time, but watch carefully for any deterioration (as occurred in Janice) that suggests a need for more urgent professional attention. Change your responses to your teen using the approach we describe, and see what happens. You can also use the book in conjunction with therapy your teen might be receiving from a mental health professional.

Specific goals of the book include helping you:
- better understand your depressed children (ages ten to seventeen);
- facilitate your children's recovery from depression;
- facilitate your children's continuing emotional health; and
- feel effective as a parent!

As parents' relationships with their teens improve, mood problems often diminish. Even if they do not, the knowledge you gain about factors that influence teen moods will still be useful, and will allow you to better assess if and when professional help is needed.

How Can Parents Help?

Whether your child or teen* suffers with serious depressed moods as Janice did, or has only occasional mood problems, you are an important person who can help him or her cope. Adolescents are still very dependent on their parents' support, even if they don't acknowledge it. When that support is informed by current knowledge about depression and teen mood problems, it can definitely make a difference. Hearing about families in similar situations may also offer insight or comfort to you, but our main focus is helping you help your depressed adolescent.

We like a sports analogy to describe parenting adolescents with emotional problems: sometimes you can coach them on how to cope more effectively; sometimes they reject coaching or don't need it anymore and you become the cheerleader on the sidelines instead; sometimes they screw up and you become the referee who calls a penalty; sometimes they are treated unfairly and you end up arguing with the referee on their behalf; always you are a steadfast fan. And, on a lighter note, if they get really difficult, you can remind them you own the stadium too.

Who Are We?

Dr. Katharina Manassis is a child psychiatrist who specializes in treating and studying children and adolescents with anxiety, depression, or both. She uses group therapy, individual therapy, and medications in her practice, emphasizing the development of coping skills that protect children and teens from further distress and impairment. This is known as "cognitive-behavioral therapy" or "CBT" for short, and the approach described in this book is based on this type of therapy. Dr. Manassis also does parenting groups and previously authored *Keys to Parenting Your Anxious Child,* a guide for parents of anxious children.

Anne Marie Levac is an advanced practice nurse who runs groups for parents of children experiencing aggression problems and for parents of children experiencing mood problems. She also has worked with individual children and teenagers using cognitive-behavioral therapy. She provides family therapy to families in which a member has a physical or mental health-related concern.

We wrote this book based on our experiences in counseling parents of depressed children and teenagers. We include suggestions from these parents in the book, so that you can benefit from their experience as well as ours. We thank them for sharing their experiences and allowing us to share them with you. Case examples have been disguised, however, to protect individual confidentiality.

---

* The terms "child," "teen," "youth," and "adolescent" are used somewhat interchangeably in this book, because the age at which depression first appears is typically somewhere between ten and twenty years.

What Can Parents Really Do?

Parents sometimes assume that the answers are all going to come from the professionals. "We've tried everything and nothing has worked" is a common refrain. Nevertheless, parents know their children better than anyone else does. Parents have spent more time with their children than anyone else. Parents have a wealth of experience with their children that nobody else shares. For these reasons, professional advice without parents' input is often useless. *Parents and professionals must work as partners in helping depressed children and teens.*

Can Parents Make a Difference in Teen Mood Problems?

Based on studies to date, we know that one or two educational sessions for parents of depressed children are of very little benefit. We also know, however, that more extensive work that includes a problem-solving approach does make a significant difference in the outcome of anxious children (they cope better when their parents are involved in treatment). Also, children who are at risk for depression (because of a depressed family member) do substantially better when the family is helped to design a plan for dealing with problems that relate to depression.

Studies of problem-solving approaches with parents of depressed adolescents are currently being done. In these studies, depressed teens are provided either traditional psychotherapy alone, or psychotherapy with a parent group focused on problem-solving. They are assigned to these two treatments randomly (like tossing a coin), to make sure that equal numbers of mildly and severely affected teens are participating in each treatment. If teens in the treatment program that includes parents do better, this result will demonstrate that parents can make a difference in their teens' recovery and should be included more regularly in treatment programs. Because many adolescents must participate to obtain conclusive results, however, it will take several years before the results are available.

Regardless of what the research has shown, in our clinical experience we have found that parents who work closely with us and with their child are more likely to see positive changes than parents who are not involved or who believe they have little influence. Parents who educate themselves about their teen's depression become better equipped to understand and help manage it. Even older adolescents (who often seemingly push their parents away from being involved) are more likely to learn positive coping strategies when parents understand, employ, and model useful coping strategies. Children benefit when parents can empathize with them, supportively challenge negative thinking, and teach them effective ways to express their feelings and try new coping strategies.

In summary, simply providing information to parents about depression seems to do little, but taking the time to *apply* the information to your particular family using a problem-solving approach like the one described in this book could probably help a lot. Children do not get depressed in a vacuum and thus it is critical to examine:

1. family relationships that may inadvertently be influencing the depression, and
2. family relationships that contribute to a child's recovery.

In the past, psychologists and psychiatrists focused excessively on parents' potential for causing depression and other emotional problems in their children. This was unfair for a couple of reasons. First, we know that there are biochemical factors (totally separate from family relationships) that contribute to depression. Second, we know that family relationships evolve over time and no one thing or no one person makes another person depressed.

Blaming the parent or blaming the teen is not helpful to recovery. Families interact in circular ways. Family members may be unaware of their influences on each other *and* unaware that changing how they interact with each other can profoundly influence the child's depression (see Chapters 12 and 13). In recent years, we have come to recognize that parents can be an important part of the *solution* to children's emotional problems. It is these solutions that are the focus of this book.

L.E.A.P. Approach

The particular problem-solving approach we describe in this book is summarized by the acronym "L.E.A.P." We chose this acronym to emphasize the need for parents and teens to move forward as they actively work together when tackling mood problems. The L.E.A.P. approach is described in more detail in Chapters 5 and 6, after the chapters describing the nature of mood problems in teens. The remainder of the book helps you apply the L.E.A.P. approach to different situations with your teen in order to help him or her overcome depressed moods.

For Janice, her mother's use of the L.E.A.P. approach was one part of a larger treatment plan developed together with a mental health professional. For children and teens with severe depression, this is usually the case. Nevertheless, L.E.A.P. dramatically improved the relationship Janice had with her mother, and allowed her mother to foster Janice's progress rather than "feeding in" to her tendency to dwell on negative thoughts. Overcoming negative thinking is a crucial task for everyone trying to recover from depression. How her mother helped is described in detail in Chapter 9.

Likewise, Mark's parents successfully applied the L.E.A.P. approach to help him get back on track at school. They addressed Mark's isolation from peers and his declining interest in school. Mark's belief that other kids disliked him was so entrenched that it prevented him from having any positive peer interaction. His parents helped Mark to label his feelings and start to notice positive moments at school. With their support, he eventually joined a photography club at school, and gained some recognition for his talent in this area. Although it took a lot of work, Mark was able to shift some of his negative thoughts about himself and others. As he was able to notice even the smallest positive step, he gradually felt better about himself and gained confidence in his ability to make and keep friends.

Kayla's mother and stepfather were determined to help Kayla out of her "slump" (as they called it) and applied the L.E.A. P. approach to simply get her out of her room! They were able to limit time spent in her room and balance it with family time in the evenings. Most of all, her stepfather found that by examining his own feelings (frustration, anger, guilt), he was better able to talk with Kayla and understand her feelings of "aloneness." After giving it some thought, he suggested to Kayla that he would drive her and a couple of friends to their riding lessons each Saturday. Kayla appreciated his support of her interest in horses, and talking with her friends in the car eased Kayla's transition back into her peer group.

How to Use the Book

The book can be used as a source of information about depression in teens, as a parent workbook to aid their teen's recovery (by following the L.E.A.P. exercises), or as both. If your child has been depressed in the past, you may wish to read the book without following the exercises, paying particular attention to ideas about reducing the risk of relapse and fostering continuing emotional health. If your child is currently depressed or you suspect depression may be present, we strongly suggest doing both. In addition, assessment by a mental health professional is also indicated if your child appears to have severe depression, such as Janice experienced. Applying the ideas in the book will make a bigger difference than just reading it! You'll also find you remember the ideas in the book more easily after you work with them.

Applying the Ideas

If you choose to do the exercises in the book, we suggest doing about one chapter a week. You can read the initial six chapters more quickly, as they are largely informational, but a chapter a week works well once you are implementing the L.E.A.P. program. Besides reading the chapter, you will need ten to fifteen minutes each week to do the exercises. This sounds very brief, but it is surprising how difficult it can be for busy parents to find that amount of uninterrupted time consistently. Each chapter will include a reminder about evaluating how the previous week's exercise went, to allow you to learn from the experience and "fine tune" what you're doing. The benefit of doing one chapter a week (instead of more) is that it gives you time to reflect on each topic and to both develop and effectively evaluate how your plan turned out.

In each chapter, there is a brief review of a specific topic illustrated with one or more case examples. Later, you are encouraged to do a problem-solving exercise based on your experiences in situations with your teen that relate to the topic. At the end of each chapter, you will find "Key Points" on a separate page, a handy summary. Some parents use them as quick reminders when they've read the book and want to review a particular topic. Others prefer to photocopy them and attach them to the refrigerator. Books are sometimes misplaced, but this rarely happens to refrigerators.

As you progress through the exercises, your teen may notice that you are responding differently in certain situations and may question your motives. It's fine to tell him or her that you are using the book. Don't defend the book too vigorously, though, or expect your teen to read it. Instead, take an experimental approach. Say something like "I'm going to try this approach for a few weeks, to see if it helps us."

The Approach in Brief

What is the L.E.A.P. approach about? Briefly, we help you develop plans for specific situations where you interact with your teen. Cognitive-behavioral therapy, the type of therapy shown effective with depressed teens, is very focused on specific situations. Its basic premise is that feelings change when people do things differently and think differently in those situations. Eventually, feelings change more generally, but change can only begin one situation at a time.

The L.E.A.P. approach encourages you to make a mental note of situations that are particularly difficult for you and your teen. Then, you are encouraged to examine your feelings in that situation, and the feelings you think your teen is having (we call this "empathy"). Using this frame of reference, you then respond to the situation using different actions (doing things differently) and different attitudes (thinking differently) than those you have used in the past. Finally, you are reminded to evaluate progress on a regular basis and revise your approach if necessary.

What to Expect

Don't expect to see much change the first six to eight weeks. Old habits die hard, and it usually takes six weeks just to begin doing things differently. For example, most people do not keep their New Year's resolutions unless they persevere past Valentine's Day (about six weeks). In addition, you will need to allow some time for your teen to get used to the new approach and to begin to realize that you're serious about it. If you see a *little* change at six to eight weeks, that's a good sign. Our clinical program of cognitive-behavioral therapy for depressed teens and their parents runs for fifteen weeks, and we do not expect to see the full benefit until the end of that time. Some teens and parents benefit sooner, however.

Please remember, though, that this book cannot replace assessment and treatment. It can be used on its own only for the mildly "moody" teen. More seriously depressed teens like Janice still need a qualified mental health professional to develop an individualized treatment plan. **Also, if at any time you fear for your teen's safety, do not hesitate to go to your nearest emergency department immediately.**

We know that coping with a depressed teen can be very difficult for parents. It is not easy to see a gradual decline in a previously outgoing, happy child or a sudden shift in a teen's mood, behavior, or appearance. It is not uncommon for parents to feel a range of emotions themselves as they are trying to understand and cope with teen

depression. However, the good news is that there are ways to make a difference. We've been using this approach for a number of years and have seen it benefit hundreds of families. We hope it will do the same for you.

Part

1

Understanding Teenage Moods

From Sadness to Suicidality:
The Spectrum of Teen Depression

Feeling sad from time to time is normal for people of all ages. Feeling depressed is not. What's the difference?

Sadness is an unpleasant emotion in response to certain events in our lives. Loss of a loved one or close friend, disappointment at missing a hoped-for opportunity, or struggling to adapt to sudden unwelcome changes, all result in sadness for most of us. Even seeing someone else experience these events in a movie can bring us to tears. Often, the tears, the grieving, the process of getting through the sadness bring relief. We take some time to stop our daily routine, reflect on what has happened, cry, and gradually replenish our energy so we can carry on. This is a healthy process.

Depression is not healthy. Depressed mood, a major symptom of depression, occurs when sadness is partnered with a change in how we perceive ourselves and others. We tend to think less of ourselves than usual. We can't forgive ourselves the slightest mistake. We see others as cold and uncaring. We can't appreciate partial success, or see the silver lining in the cloud. We feel helpless and defeated. We can't imagine facing life's challenges and going on. In short, sadness repairs while depression impairs.

We shouldn't expect our children to be free from sadness. In fact, denying sadness or grief in ourselves or others can cause emotional problems. We should, however, expect our children to be free from depression. The occasional down mood occurs in most teens. Ongoing depression does not. How, as a parent, can you tell the difference? In truth, there is no single test that will tell you. In part, this is because teens don't tell you everything that goes on in their minds. They shouldn't be expected to. A certain amount of privacy is part of growing up and becoming your own person. In part, this is because there is a whole range or "spectrum" of experiences between uncomplicated sadness and clinical depression.

This book discusses teens all the way along that spectrum. The approach described applies to any teen whose sadness is complicated by feelings of low self-worth, overly negative appraisals of events, helplessness, or hopelessness. In more severe cases, it serves as an adjunct to clinical treatments. In milder depressive states, it may allow you to get your teen back to a more average frame of mind, appropriate to his or her stage of development. Before discussing how to do this, however, let's examine some of the depressive states along the spectrum. Think about which one (or ones) might apply to your teen. In this chapter, we illustrate some of the more common, milder depressive conditions. In the next chapter, conditions on the more severe end of the spectrum (Dysthymic Disorder, Major Depression, Bipolar Disorder) are discussed.

Acute Depressive Conditions

Sometimes depressed mood starts suddenly, in response to a stressful event. There are two such "acute" depressive conditions recognized by mental health professionals. These are: Adjustment Disorder with Depressed Mood and Grief Reaction(s).

Adjustment Disorder with Depressed Mood

Nadine: *Nadine had a gift for music. Everyone encouraged her to nurture this talent. When the opportunity came along to attend a special high school for the performing arts, there was no doubt that this was where Nadine belonged. Unfortunately, none of Nadine's friends were able to join her at the new school. They all were enrolled in the college preparatory program at the local high school. She missed them terribly, and found it harder than she expected to fit in with her new, artistic peers. Furthermore, at her old school, she was praised regularly for her exceptional talent. At the new school, she actually lagged behind her peers in some areas. Many of them had performed in recitals for years and were already entering professional competitions. Rather than feeling privileged to attend the school, Nadine felt like a fish out of water. She regretted deciding to go there. She became sullen and discouraged as she dragged herself to school every morning. By October, she was skipping classes and withdrawing from peers and family.*

In this case, a teen is experiencing a very distressing event that is not extreme enough to be considered a trauma, but nevertheless profoundly affects her mood. School changes or breaking up with a boyfriend or girlfriend, for example, are common triggers of depressed moods. When the depressed mood persists for a month or more, this is called an adjustment disorder. Although unpleasant, adjustment disorders are usually not accompanied by the disturbances of sleep, appetite, energy, and concentration, nor by the extreme hopelessness or extremely low self-worth characteristic of major depression. In an adjustment disorder, the change in mood is entirely related to the distressing event, and tends to resolve as the teen adjusts to the new reality (usually, a few days to a few weeks at the most) and finds new sources of enjoyment.

In Nadine's case, for example, she contacted some of her old friends and found out about the struggles they faced at their new school. Her predicament didn't seem so uniquely difficult, and she found comfort in commiserating with them. Eventually, she found a sympathetic teacher at the new school who encouraged her to write for the yearbook, and the peers involved in this activity became her friends. In some cases, supportive counseling is needed to help teens adapt.

If your son or daughter experiences mood changes related to a distressing event, try to provide comfort while maintaining normal routines. If the mood change persists for several months, or you think there might be a risk of self-harm, have him seen by a doctor to clarify the diagnosis and assess whether or not treatment is needed.

Grief Reaction

Tyler: *Tyler's parents had divorced when he was a toddler, and his mother remarried when he was ten. Now fourteen, Tyler had never gotten along with his stepfather, and his older sisters tended to pick on him. He always looked forward to Sundays, though. On Sundays, he visited his grandfather, Bill. Grandpa Bill knew more about baseball than anyone Tyler had ever met, and could describe key moments of every World Series going back to the '40s. Tyler shared his passion. Sometimes, they'd get to watch a game together. Other times, they just went through Grandpa's baseball cards, autographed balls, and other memorabilia and the stories they brought to mind. Grandpa Bill was determined to live alone, even though his health was failing.*

One day, Tyler's mother looked very serious. Gently, she tried to break the shocking news to him: his grandfather had had a stroke. He wasn't expected to recover. Three days later, he passed away and Tyler was inconsolable. He had nothing to look forward to anymore. He pined in his room for days. Eventually, his mother suggested he write a tribute to his grandfather for the local newspaper. He was proud to do it. With more encouragement, he began to volunteer to pass out programs when his town's team played a home game. He had never been a great player, but his knowledge of the game soon made him a fixture behind the bench. He set a goal of becoming a sportscaster one day.

Like Nadine, Tyler had to adjust to a major life change. Loss of a key person in a teen's life can be devastating, especially if unexpected. For Tyler, his grandfather's role was doubly important because of the more strained relationships he had with other family members. It was not going to be possible to replace his grandfather, as it rarely is when the lost person is significant. Instead, he had to find a way to honor his memory, maintain an important aspect of the relationship in his life (in this case, the love of baseball), and go on. Fortunately, his mother was sensitive to these issues and helped him grieve appropriately.

As adults, we should never assume that a loss is insignificant to a teen. Apparently distant friends or relatives, even pets, can be missed terribly. Even a famous person the teen admires (for example, a famous musician or actor) can be mourned, especially if that person symbolizes an important aspect of the teen's emerging identity. Don't be shy about asking how your teen's life is different, now that the person is gone. The answer may surprise you. If a grief reaction is prolonged or accompanied by symptoms suggestive of more serious depression, counseling should be sought.

Chronic Depressive Conditions

"Chronic depressive conditions" is a term for conditions that involve longstanding depressed mood not directly related to a specific incident or set of circumstances. Three examples of chronic depressive conditions will now be described.

Difficult Temperament

Lexy: *Lexy had always been considered a "high maintenance" child. She made frequent, loud demands for attention as an infant, and had continued to do so for much of her life. She ate irregularly and slept irregularly, despite numerous attempts by her family to establish routines. She pouted miserably when things were the slightest bit different from what she expected. She insisted on being in charge when playing with her friends. She had difficulty adjusting to high school, where she had to rotate from class to class and had a different teacher in each subject. She became preoccupied with her teachers' different teaching styles, insisting that some were simply wrong. Similarly, her peers could never measure up to her exacting standards, and she soon had a very small circle of friends. If anyone commented on how she was making herself miserable, she blamed that person for the problem.*

Some children seem to be born with the proverbial "cloud over their heads." They rarely smile, have trouble controlling themselves emotionally and physiologically (for example, sleeping and eating irregularly), and seem to be constantly making demands on others. Perhaps in response to their poor internal control, they try too hard to control their environments, resulting in inflexibility and difficulty dealing with change. This so-called difficult temperament can persist, to a degree, for most of their lives unless they learn alternative ways of coping. Children with difficult temperament can do very well in certain circumstances. For example, stubbornness that is appropriately channeled can contribute to success. Consequently, these children are not considered to have a disorder. Nevertheless, they suffer from their own difficulty adapting, and sometimes become depressed when faced with the challenges of adolescence.

Low Self-Esteem

Carlos: *Carlos always seemed to live in the shadow of his older brother, Joe. Joe was an excellent basketball player, top student, and popular among his peers. Carlos was none of these. He was constantly trying to impress his friends with feats of daring, often injuring himself in the process. They merely laughed. Carlos bragged about his computer game system. The other boys thought he was showing off. Their families couldn't afford the latest systems. Inside, Carlos was miserable: constantly comparing himself to others and feeling that he didn't measure up. His stunts and bragging were ineffective ways of looking for praise.*

Self-esteem may be defined as confidence in and satisfaction with oneself (Merriam Webster online dictionary). Self-esteem is an odd concept: those who have it, rarely think about it; those who don't, are preoccupied with their lack of it. Adolescence predisposes teens to self-esteem problems because teens are often self-conscious. They feel that others are watching them and evaluating them more than is realistic. This self-consciousness is part of the healthy adolescent quest for individual identity. For some teens, however, it can result in unfavorable comparisons with others, such as what Carlos experienced. These teens suffer low moods related to their constant focus on self-worth or their perceived lack of it. Family problems or rejection by others can compound the problem.

What these teens need to develop is a sense of being valuable and loveable just as they are (regardless of the latest comparison or competition). Thus, finding an activity they excel at is only part of the answer. Accepting them, laughing with them (never at them), and normalizing some of the self-absorption of youth are equally important. Taking the focus off comparisons with others, and instead emphasizing "being the best you can be" is helpful. Also, parents can show by example that it is possible to have fun regardless of whether you are "winning" or "losing" in a given activity. Teens can learn that life is much more enjoyable when we focus on the moment, rather than ourselves.

Depressed Mood Related to Difficult Life Circumstances

Benny: *Benny's family lived on social assistance. His father had left the family years ago because of alcohol problems. His mother had not been able to find work, and had three young boys to raise. They didn't have medical insurance, so he and his siblings often suffered through ear infections or sore throats without antibiotics. Their sneakers were often falling apart by the time their mother could replace them. Benny was embarrassed by all this, and lied to his friends about his home life. His mother was upset that he was ashamed of his family, and smacked him roughly when she heard. Unlike his two younger brothers, he always seemed to be in some sort of trouble. When there was a fight among the boys, Benny usually got blamed. He often thought he should run away from home, but there was nowhere safe to go. He didn't want to end* *up in a gang like some of the other boys in his neighborhood, but he often wondered how else to find a place to fit in.*

Benny's life has been difficult from the start. He is not faced with adjusting to a sudden change, but rather coping and trying to make a good life for himself despite the odds. His environment poses a combination of several risk factors for maladjustment. Poverty, a rough neighborhood, a stressed single-parent household, limited access to medical care, less than optimal parenting, and being made the scapegoat in the family can all contribute to emotional problems. Benny does not necessarily need counseling. Benny needs a source of hope for the future. The ability to excel in some area that would allow him to escape his circumstances would strengthen this. A successful male role model that took an interest in him (for example, a big brother) could also be helpful. Emotional support for his mother could also, indirectly, benefit Benny and his brothers. Although helpful interventions in this case are more social than psychiatric, they are no less important if Benny is to have a chance to make it.

What If Your Teen Appears to be Deteriorating?

Importantly, none of the conditions described above are permanent states. Any one of them can change over time and progress toward more serious depression or toward emotional health. If you think your child may be more depressed than the teens profiled in this chapter, or if you think your child is deteriorating in that direction, see the next chapter for a fuller discussion about assessing teens for depression. If your teen is experiencing depression, you will need to seek professional help. Start by checking with your family doctor to determine whether a medical condition might account for your teen's mood. If not, ask the doctor to refer your teen to a mental health professional in your area.

Depressed Mood Secondary to Other Problems

Sometimes teens experience depressed moods that are associated with ("secondary to") other problems such as medical problems or psychological problems. It does not mean that their symptoms are not serious or concerning, it means that they are caused by different factors. In order to treat the problem accurately and effectively, it is important for it to be properly diagnosed.

Depressed Mood Related to Medical Problems

Several specific medical conditions can result in depression. In addition, struggling with any chronic illness can become discouraging and depressing over time.

Recognizing medical conditions that cause depression is important because treating them appropriately may avoid long, ineffective courses of psychotherapy or antidepressant therapy. Most can be ruled out by a family doctor doing a history, physical examination, and (in some cases) blood tests.

There is no physical test for depression itself, however (see pages 28-29). There are literally hundreds of diseases and medications that can affect mood, so only some of the more common ones found in teens will be listed here:

- *Hypothyroidism* (low function of the thyroid gland) can mimic depression. Weight gain, sluggishness, sensitivity to the cold, and dry skin often accompany this condition.
- *Infectious mononucleosis* (the so-called "kissing disease," caused by a virus) is another common cause of fatigue and low mood in teens.
- *Poor eating habits* can result in anemia (not enough red blood cells), with associated fatigue and low mood.
- *A variety of drugs* (whether prescription, over-the-counter, or street drugs) can affect mood. Teens who are drinking alcohol regularly, for example, often go through cycles of intoxication and withdrawal that disturb their moods.
- *Starting the birth control pill* can result in hormonal changes that induce depressed moods in some girls. For similar reasons, premenstrual depressed mood occurs in others.
- *Chronically ill teens taking corticosteroids* (for example, for rheumatic diseases or chronic kidney or liver conditions) can experience mood disturbance, with either elation or depression.
- *Finally, medical conditions resulting in disability* can be depressing. Accidents that result in sudden disability (for example, diving accidents resulting in paralysis) can be especially devastating because they rob the teen of previously cherished hopes and dreams.

Depressed Mood Related to Other Psychological Problems

Certain problems cluster together in families, suggesting that children vulnerable to one may be more vulnerable to the others. Depression, anxiety, and alcoholism have all been linked in this way. Therefore, teens with anxiety or alcohol problems often manifest depression as well. Other psychological problems can also overlap, when they are chronic and untreated. Children with undiagnosed attention problems or learning disabilities, for example, can become increasingly discouraged over time as they are unable to succeed academically. Children with behavioral problems often receive negative feedback, until they come to see themselves as "nothing but trouble." This negative identity certainly predisposes teens to depression.

What Next?

If you are pretty sure your child has one of the problems described in this chapter, this book will help you develop some useful plans to help you and your teen better manage his depressed mood. However, if you believe that your teen may be experiencing a more serious mood disorder such as major depression, bipolar disorder, or dysthymic disorder (see next chapter), then we recommend a trip to the family doctor to rule out any medical condition that may be affecting his mood and/or to make a referral to a mental health professional for treatment.

Is the Approach from this Book Working?

If you choose to work with this book to help your teen overcome depressed moods, you may have to be patient. Changes in teens' emotions and behaviors take time to develop and may go "two steps forward and one step back." Sometimes a teen is making progress slowly, but it's difficult to notice. In order to help you notice gradual change and to avoid discouragement, we suggest rating each of the items on page 11 on a scale from 1 to 4 before you try to implement any of the suggestions in this book.

> 1 = almost never
> 2 = sometimes
> 3 = often
> 4 = almost always

Later on, you can rate your teen again and see if he is making improvement. Lower scores represent improvement!

Items are based on accepted diagnostic criteria for depression and on some common areas of impairment in depressed teens.

Statement	Rating
1. My teen's mood is generally sad or irritable.	☐
2. My teen doesn't seem to enjoy activities he/she used to like.	☐
3. My teen eats much more or much less than before.	☐
4. My teen sleeps much more or much less than before.	☐
5. My teen seems really "slowed down."	☐
6. My teen seems really "revved up."	☐
7. My teen seems to have no energy for anything.	☐
8. My teen puts himself down a lot.	☐
9. My teen feels excessively guilty about things.	☐
10. My teen complains about his/her body.	☐
11. My teen can't focus on his/her schoolwork.	☐
12. My teen seems hopeless about the future.	☐
13. My teen questions the value of life.*	☐
14. My teen avoids going out with friends.	☐
15. My teen avoids communicating with friends.	☐
16. My teen avoids participating in family activities.	☐
17. My teen avoids communicating with family members.	☐
18. My teen stays alone in his/her room.	☐
19. My teen avoids going to school.	☐
20. My teen does worse than before at school.	☐

The list above is by no means exhaustive. Therefore, if you have noticed a change in your teen that is not listed but seems to be connected to negative mood, add it in and rate it from 1 to 4 as well.

---

* This suggests more urgent need for professional assessment.

Key Points

Conditions on the Depressive Spectrum include:

- Adjustment Disorders (in response to recent stress)
- Grief Reactions
- Low Self-Esteem
- Difficult Temperament
- Coping with Difficult Life Circumstances
- Depression Secondary to Medical Problems
- Depression Secondary to Other Psychological Problems

Of the above, which one(s) apply to your teen? Why do you think so? If in doubt, seek a doctor's advice.

_____

_____

_____

_____

_____

_____

_____

_____

_____

Causes and Treatments of Depression:
An Overview

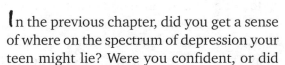

In the previous chapter, did you get a sense of where on the spectrum of depression your teen might lie? Were you confident, or did you ask a professional or someone else for another opinion? If you didn't recognize your teen in any of the examples given in Chapter 1, she may have a more serious form of depression or another condition altogether. This chapter discusses the types of teen depression that are considered clinically important, and likely to result in a need for professional help. It also touches on some other conditions that may need to be ruled out since they can cause symptoms similar to those seen in depression.

Timothy: *Timothy, age thirteen, had always been more difficult to raise than his siblings. He was very demanding of his parents and often picky about the foods he would eat and the clothes he would wear. He was easily irritated by minor changes in routine. He had temper "blow-ups" on a regular basis, despite his parents' administration of calm, consistent time-outs. He made friends without difficulty, but had trouble keeping them because his peers perceived him as being too bossy.*

Timothy had never been a good student, but lately his grades had been worse than usual. Last year's teacher suggested an assessment for Attention-Deficit/Hyperactivity Disorder (AD/HD) or a learning disability. The psychologist who saw Timothy clearly did not think either of these diagnoses explained his difficulties. Timothy was not particularly distractible or impulsive, and his academic ability was above average in all areas. He did, however, become frustrated very easily when he was unable to master a task on the first try, responding with "I'm no good at anything!" and slamming the book shut. Timothy's difficulty was thought to be due to an emerging mood disorder.

Timothy's main risk factor for mood problems was his very difficult temperament. His parents were sympathetic, but they found his behavior frustrating at times. "The parenting courses helped, but they're not enough for dealing with this one!" reported his mother. As Timothy's temperament began to affect his functioning at school and with peers, his mood declined.

Interestingly, there was no major stress that seemed to prompt his deterioration in the previous year. More likely, he was simply struggling with society's increased expectations of more "mature" behavior with increasing age. For most people, maturity is seen as the ability to persevere despite adversity, and show a certain amount of flexibility and consideration for others. These behaviors would be difficult for Timothy to develop, given his rigid temperament and low frustration tolerance.

Defining Depression

Compare Janice (in the Introduction) and Timothy for a moment. Although both suffer from low moods and are about the same age, there are significant differences between them (apart from gender). Janice functioned very well, until a relatively sudden decline in her mood occurred over a couple of months. Timothy, on the other hand, had always struggled to a degree, but developed increasing difficulties over a year or so. Once depressed mood set in, however, Janice had many more symptoms than Timothy. Her appetite, sleep, energy level, and ability to concentrate were all affected by depression. She expressed feelings of worthlessness and no longer enjoyed her previous activities. Timothy's sleep was disturbed and he made some self-deprecating remarks, but the change in his mood and behavior was far less dramatic than that of Janice.

Janice exemplifies major depression, a diagnosis made when people become dramatically impaired by depressed moods over a relatively short period of time. Timothy, on the other hand, exemplifies dysthymic disorder, a diagnosis given when people have some impairment, but to a lesser degree than in major depression. They typically experience a chronically low mood and their problems occur over a longer time period (usually a year or more). A third consideration in teens is whether changes in mood or behavior are part of a disorder or part of normal adolescence. This question will be examined in Chapter 4.

Major Depression

About 5 percent of children and adolescents in the general population suffer from major depression at any given point in time (American Academy of Child and Adolescent psychiatry, www.aacap.org). Major depression, also known as a clinical depression, is not a single symptom but rather a cluster of symptoms. Major depression is most likely to be present if there has been a change in the teen's patterns of thoughts, feelings, and/or behaviors which are manifested with the following symptoms:

- Frequent sadness or "down" mood
- Increased irritability, anger, or hostility (sometimes children exhibit more irritability than sadness with depression)
- Lack of enjoyment (also called "anhedonia") or inability to enjoy activities that the teen previously showed interest in
- Appetite change (either an increase or decrease in appetite)
- Sleep change (difficulty falling asleep, restless sleep, sleeping more or less than usual)
- Low energy
- Low concentration
- Motor agitation (such as restlessness, fidgeting or pacing, or reporting feeling "revved up") or slowing down (such as feeling as if daily activities are hard to get through or to physically complete)
- Guilt or worthlessness (such as feeling or expressing guilt or feeling worthless or "like a loser")
- Suicidality (ranging from questioning the value of life, to actual thoughts, expressions, or gestures of self-harm (refer to Chapter 14)
- Depressed adolescents may also abuse drugs or alcohol as a way to make themselves feel better.

A diagnosis of major depression will be made if the teen's feelings of sadness and lack of enjoyment have gone on for at least two weeks and if four or more of the other listed symptoms have occurred almost every day. Suicidal thoughts and feelings may not occur as frequently as daily. However, if they exist at all, they need to be explored immediately.

There can be a genetic component to depression. One study (Kovacs, 1997) showed that families of depressed teens were five times as likely as those of non-depressed teens to have a person in the family who also suffered from depression. The closer the relative is, the higher the risk.

Depressed children and teens have most of these symptoms for at least a couple of weeks. Briefer mood disturbances sometimes occur in response to stress, but this is not considered true "clinical depression" (i.e., a depression requiring treatment). Everyone has these symptoms sometimes (for example, normal grief), but if they persist and interfere with day-to-day functioning, they constitute a disorder.

Once a disorder is diagnosed, it can happen once (a so-called "single episode" of depression), or several times (called "recurrent depression"). A single episode can last anywhere from a few months to a year. Therefore, it is important that professional involvement continues for at least this length of time. A substantial number of depressed teens (30 to 40 percent) have recurrent depression, so it is important to watch for further mood problems once an episode of depression resolves. Early intervention can minimize the impact of recurrent episodes of depression. Without intervention, a teen's self-esteem and ability to function (in the family, socially, academically) can be severely affected.

A teen who experiences a major mood disorder with hallucinations (such as hearing voices) or delusions (such as having unrealistic ideas about a TV show containing a special message for her), but does not have schizophrenia, may be experiencing psychotic depression. **These teens often need treatment in a hospital, and are at high risk of another condition—bipolar disorder** (see below).

Bipolar Disorder

Mania is having the opposite picture to depression for at least a week (for example, high energy, fast speech, elated mood, involvement in reckless activities), sometimes accompanied by feelings of grandiosity (being better than everyone else). It occurs in a subgroup of depressed teens, and is also known as "bipolar illness" or "bipolar affective disorder." In bipolar illness, episodes of depression and episodes of mania both occur at different times. Between episodes, the teen may appear normal and function well. It is important to tell your child's doctor if there is a family history of mania as well as depression, as this may affect the treatment plan. (For example, the choice of medication is sometimes different with this information.)

There is a genetic predisposition to bipolar disorder. If the teen has an immediate family member diagnosed with bipolar, there is about a 4.5 percent chance of the child getting bipolar disorder and about a 14 percent chance of getting major depression.

In teens and children, bipolar disorder is sometimes difficult to distinguish from AD/HD and other childhood disorders. Therefore, it requires a thorough diagnostic assessment, and sometimes further assessment of mood patterns over time, before the diagnosis is clear.

Because teens who are manic can engage in dangerous activities and/or lose their perspective on reality, have your teen see a doctor immediately if you think she has this problem. The approach described in this book is *not* suitable for helping teens overcome manic states. The approach can still be used, however, to help these teens with their depressed states.

Dysthymic Disorder

Dysthymic disorder or dysthymia (pronounced "dis-THI-me-uh) is a type of depression that is less severe than major depression. It is characterized by long-term chronic symptoms that keep individuals from functioning with usual energy levels and from feeling good. There are fewer physical symptoms than with major depression, but more emotional symptoms such as gloomy thoughts and low mood (Kaufman, 2000). Sometimes people with dysthymia also experience major depressive episodes, so it is worth watching for signs that this is happening. If a major depressive episode is occurring, the teen's moods will be clearly worse than usual and she will experience more physical symptoms than usual.

> **Descriptions by Parents of Depressed Teens**
>
> - "She just seems angry with the world."
> - "He's always got the door shut, like he is doing a secret experiment in there."
> - "Some days I want to light a fire under him! He just doesn't move."
> - "When the kids tease her, she just takes it. She won't fight back."
> - "Whenever I suggest doing something he used to like, he just says 'So what?'"

Causes of Depression

As in most mental illnesses, we can't really talk about a single "cause" in depression. There are usually both constitutional (inborn) and environmental factors that contribute to the condition, and often there are one or more environmental stresses (such as school demands and frustrations, death of a loved one, a move, or separation or divorce of parents) that act as triggers for a particular depressive episode. As a parent, blaming yourself or your spouse for your son's or daughter's condition is unlikely to be helpful. It is worthwhile having a thorough assessment by a mental health professional, however, as this may clarify the diagnosis and uncover contributing factors that could be changed. Information about seeking professional help is discussed in Chapter 4.

Some teens are initially thought to be depressed but are later found to be suffering from a medical condition that is producing mood changes. Thyroid problems and anemia (low iron in the blood) commonly cause mood changes, but so too may other medical conditions. Use of certain medications (for example, birth control pills) or street drugs can also affect mood. If your teen hasn't had a recent physical examination, it is well worth pursuing one. Remember to tell the doctor about the mood changes so he or she knows what to look for.

Parents often inquire about blood tests or other examinations that could reveal whether or not their child's brain chemistry is abnormal. Unfortunately, measuring brain chemicals in the bloodstream is not reliable, as there is a cellular barrier or wall between the bloodstream and the brain. Thus, levels of brain chemicals in the bloodstream do not necessarily reflect similar levels in the brain. Brain structure is rarely abnormal in depression, so computerized tomography (CT scan) or magnetic resonance imaging (MRI scan) usually do not help. Brain functioning, as measured by positron emission tomography (PET scan), can be abnormal, but such scans are very expensive, and are usually only available as part of research protocols.

Reactions to traumatic events (so-called "post-traumatic stress disorder") can also mimic depression. Although we all try to protect our children as best we can, it's impossible to monitor teens twenty-four hours a day, so the possibility of a traumatic event should not be dismissed too quickly. Children with pre-existing mental health problems such as anxiety disorders or attention-deficit/hyperactivity disorder are also more vulnerable to developing depression in adolescence.

Note that some things that used to be considered causes of depression are now recognized as part of the illness (for example, pessimistic thinking, social withdrawal, or a tendency to ruminate on past mistakes). Depressed people typically withdraw and see the "glass half empty." Most brief, focused psychotherapies address these symptoms early, by encouraging constructive action and realistically positive thinking. Feelings often take longer to change.

Common Contributing Factors

Genes

Genes are materials in the cell that determine our physical and other characteristics such as eye color, height, and blood type and are passed on from one generation to the next. Probably several genes are involved in depression, and families with histories of alcohol or anxiety problems also carry a higher risk of depression. This does not mean that if a parent has depression (or bipolar disorder), that the child will have depression (or bipolar). In fact, when a first-degree relative of a child (parent or sibling) has depression, there is a 1.5 percent chance of the child being depressed and 16 percent chance they will have bipolar disorder. Likewise, if a first-degree relative has bipolar disorder, the child has a 4.5 percent chance of becoming bipolar and a 14 percent chance of experiencing depression. The bottom line is, most children of depressed parents do *not* become depressed, but they are at higher risk than the average child.

Brain Chemicals

A number of brain chemicals, or neurotransmitters, help brain cells communicate with one another. Serotonin and norepinephrine are two such chemicals, and people who are depressed tend to have lower than average levels of these chemicals in certain parts of the brain. Because medications that increase levels of either of these chemicals tend to be helpful in about 80 percent of depressed people, we conclude that many people have a biological basis for their depression. However, these brain chemicals are also influenced by environmental factors. Children who are abused, for example, can have altered brain chemistry associated with their abuse.

Kindling

Once the brain gets used to thinking in depressed ways, it becomes progressively easier to slip into these depressed thinking patterns in response to problems. This "kindling" (or tendency for commonly used thinking styles to become automatic) is one reason why early treatment of depression is so important!

Life Stress

Most people respond to stress with a "fight or flight" response, to either deal with the stress or escape it. Depression occurs in reaction to stress only when the stress is either: 1) too great to deal with (for example, a major loss); or 2) repeated and perceived to be inescapable (termed "learned helplessness"). Stress often acts as a trigger for an episode of depression.

Learned Helplessness

Learned helplessness (the perception that stress is inescapable) is particularly problematic, because it interferes with the desire to help oneself. After all, what's the point in trying to change things if you can't reduce the stress anyway? Eventually, this attitude leads to hopelessness and despair. Some theorists link most or all depression to this state of mind.

In most cases, depression is due to a combination of several of these factors and not just one alone.

How Common Is Depression?

About 5 percent of children and teens in the general population suffer from major depression at any given point in time (www.aacap.org). The milder conditions related to depression we discussed in the last chapter are even more common. Depression tends to be more common in girls than boys after puberty, although symptoms may differ. It is not clear whether or not this gender difference is due to hormones. After all, many girls go through the hormonal changes of puberty with no significant mood problems. Some studies suggest that societal expectations of girls and women play a larger role than hormones in influencing moods.

Other Possible Causes

What about Past Experiences?

In some forms of psychotherapy, the focus is on uncovering or exploring events in the past that may have led to the person's depressed state. This information can be helpful in better understanding the current situation, but it does not necessarily change the individual's depressed mood.

The past is relevant to the extent that it affects current thoughts, feelings, and behaviors. If repeating destructive patterns can be found, these are worth examining and changing. In teens, however, such patterns are not always evident, and if they are, they often take time to change. Nevertheless, it is surprising how many people are effectively treated for depression with no need to re-examine the past or find the psychological "roots" of their depression. Many depressed people do better looking *forward* than looking back. Focusing on changing current behaviors and thoughts (a so-called "cognitive-behavioral" perspective) is a forward-looking approach to depression that has been shown to be helpful in adolescents and adults alike. In this book, which is written from a cognitive-behavioral perspective, we focus on problem solving issues that are currently occurring. (See Chapter 9 for more information about the cognitive-behavioral approach.)

What about Hormones?

Some girls and women experience depressed mood consistently at certain points in their menstrual cycle. Currently termed "premenstrual dysphoric disorder," this condition can respond to antidepressant medications. In girls with irregular cycles (common the first year or two after menstruation begins), birth control pills that regulate the cycles may regulate associated mood problems as well. Given that most girls' cycles eventually become more regular, however, our practice is to advise patience, and only provide medication when depressive symptoms are severe or do not resolve when the cycles become regular.

Sudden hormonal changes—as occur after giving birth, for example—can certainly trigger depression. Therefore, depression is particularly common in women after having a baby (so-called "postpartum depression"), especially if there has been a previous depressive episode. Because this form of depression can be particularly severe, early contact with a mental health professional is essential.

What about Lack of Sunlight?

There is a subtype of depression called Seasonal Affective Disorder (SAD) that has been linked to the lack of sun exposure people in the Northern Hemisphere experience in the winter months (and people in the Southern Hemisphere experience in the summer months). For people who consistently get depressed during seasons that lack sunshine and not at other times of the year, this diagnosis may apply. Some of these people experience improved mood when treated with photo therapy (bright lights, brighter than ordinary room lighting).

If you think your child or teen may have Seasonal Affective Disorder, talk to the doctor. However, don't leap to conclusions if your youngster is depressed in the winter. Remember: winter is associated with less sun, but also with more school. Any stress at school, whether it's academic problems, a tough teacher, or a peer problem, can contribute to depression. For this reason, talk to a professional before considering photo therapy, and only use an approved bright light device. Don't risk sunburn or eye damage by exposing your child to extra sunlight.

What Helps?: A Short Synopsis of Topics Detailed Later in the Book

Listed below is a "snapshot" of things to keep in mind to help you help your child. We will be discussing these ideas throughout the book in more detail but provide some highlights here to provide an introduction to what helps.

- *Focusing on realistic positives*—This week, use the table provided at the end of the chapter to record some areas in which your child is already showing some positive abilities, even if they are small positives (for example, getting dressed in the morning).

- *Getting active*—Activity counteracts the tendency for depressed people to withdraw and ruminate, and physical activity can actually prevent relapse in some people.
- *Taking medication (if needed)*—Medications can normalize the levels of the brain chemicals mentioned above.
- *Reducing unnecessary stress*—For example, if your teen is feeling overwhelmed by three after-school activities in addition to regular courses, see if even one can be eliminated until she is feeling better. Family conflict can also constitute "unnecessary stress." Chapters 12 and 13 are devoted to addressing family interactions.
- *Increasing perceived support*—Perceived support (that is, the child actually *feels* supported) ameliorates the effect of stress, reduces learned helplessness, and offers hope. Empathy is perceived as particularly supportive, but it's one of the most difficult things to give a depressed teen. Depression constricts the range of emotional expression, making depressed teens "hard to read." Teens' tendency to shut down and withdraw while depressed adds to the problem. Sometimes, you will have to take an educated guess about what is going on, based on the circumstances. Then, put it into words for your teen. For example, "If that happened to me, I would feel terribly angry. Is that how you're feeling?" The expression on her face will give you the answer. Expressing confidence in your teen is another aspect of perceived support. Many children and teens do better when those close to them expect that they can. Siblings may need a little extra attention too, to reduce the chances of increased sibling rivalry as you focus on helping the depressed teen.
- *Mourning major losses (if any)*—Several books on helping children and teens with grief are listed in the Bibliography.
- *Having a chance to make a difference*—Making a difference (no matter how small) helps to overcome feelings of learned helplessness. For example, something as simple as being able to continue looking after a pet can provide a sense of "making a difference."

Your Homework as Parents

Each week, starting with this one, we will provide some "homework" ideas based on each chapter. Take about fifteen minutes each week to complete this recommended activity. For this week, we encourage you to read the Key Points and complete the "Child's Abilities" chart on the following pages. Completing this chart is an important first step. You are asked to notice your child's abilities or positive steps and build on them. We encourage parents to take one step at a time. When parents take time to notice even the smallest positive, they are more able to recognize progress and feel less overwhelmed.

Key Points

- Focus on realistic positives
- Get active
- Use medication (if needed)
- Reduce unnecessary stress
- Increase perceived support
- Mourn major losses
- Make a difference (no matter how small)

This week, record some areas in which your child is already showing some positive abilities, even if they are small positives (for example, getting dressed in the morning). We have provided an example of a chart that Timothy's parents completed below, and a blank chart for you to fill out on the next page.

Child's Abilities (Realistic Positives)

FOR: Timmy

Area	Positive Abilities
Family	He did not complain during supper on Monday night
School	He worked on his homework for 30 minutes without stating that he is no good at math.
Peers	His friend Michael came over on Saturday and things went relatively well—Timothy was not bossy as he had been on a previous visit.
Self-Care	Took a shower and washed his hair on Sunday without me nagging!
Other	Timothy is really trying hard with his goal of getting along better with friends. I really noticed this on Saturday and told him so!

Child's Abilities (Realistic Positives)

FOR: _____

Area	Positive Abilities
Family	
School	
Peers	
Self-Care	
Other	

Seeking Professional Help for Your Teen

Parents are often the first to recognize the presence of emotional or behavioral problems in their child's life. If you have identified symptoms of depression through this book or through others who know and have voiced concern about your teen, we strongly advise that you seek professional help. That is not to say that the decision to seek help is an easy one. With the negative stigma of depression, it can often be difficult and painful for parents and embarrassing for adolescents. But, we believe it is worth it.

The first step is to gently try to talk to your teen. An honest, open talk about your concern might help your teen to share his thoughts and feelings with you. He needs to know that you are concerned and would like to check things out for him with a professional.

What If My Teen Won't See a Psychologist or Psychiatrist?

Many teens are leery of seeing a "shrink." When they reject psychiatric help, it is often because they are familiar with media stereotypes of mental health professionals and the people who consult them, or because they fear appearing weak in front of peers.

See if your son would consider seeing a family doctor, nurse practitioner, or school nurse first. Some teens are willing to agree to a "check-up" of physical health (for example, to look at causes for the fatigue often associated with depression) but not to an appointment focused on mental health. A sensitive nurse or physician may be able to gradually explore mental health issues either as part of the check-up or during a follow-up visit. If your teen is hesitant about seeing his usual nurse or doctor, perhaps because of confidentiality concerns, provide some alternative names. In some communities, specialized "teen clinics" are available for adolescent health concerns as well. You could also ask the school counselor to chat with your teen about what is bothering him and, perhaps, about pursuing an appointment with a psychologist or psychiatrist.

If you cannot get your teen to see anybody, ask the professional you wanted your teen to consult whether he or she would be willing to speak to you, the parent, as a first step. Just getting an outside perspective on your child's difficulties may be helpful, and may give you additional ideas on how to get him to access help.

What Professionals Can Determine Whether a Child/Teen Is Depressed?

There are many mental health professionals—psychiatrists, psychologists, nurses, nurse practitioners, social workers, child and youth workers, child care workers, child care associates, counselors, and others—who work with depressed teens. It is sometimes overwhelming to know who to seek help from!

First, we advise you to rule out any medical conditions that may be causing the depression. It is also important to clarify from the outset whether your teen is experiencing a clinical depression. In order to get a diagnosis for your teen and rule out medical factors that may be contributing to the depressed mood, it is necessary to see a child and adolescent psychiatrist. The psychiatrist is a medical doctor who will rule out medical conditions by conducting a simple physical exam and order blood tests, if indicated. He or she also has the qualifications to prescribe and monitor medications if this becomes a recommended part of treatment for your child.

If a medical doctor has already ruled out physical conditions and you want a mental health diagnosis, you could consult a registered child psychologist instead of a psychiatrist. A psychologist cannot prescribe medications in most states or Canada but can assess, diagnose, and treat the teen for depression.

Other mental health professionals listed may conduct clinical assessments using validated questionnaires to help guide their assessments. They use knowledge of biological, psychological, and social factors in working with teens and their parents. However, they do not provide a formal diagnosis. They may, however, treat a child who has already been diagnosed.

If your child will need ongoing treatment, we recommend finding a mental health professional (like those listed above) who:

- specializes in child and family mental health,
- is qualified to provide cognitive-behavioral therapy (we will be describing this evidence-based therapy approach throughout the book),
- is someone your teen will feel comfortable with and can relate to,
- is flexible, and
- is able to see your teen as an individual.

How Do I Locate a Professional?

There are different ways to locate a professional to help your child. Probably the best way is by word of mouth through family and friends or others such as teachers or members of church or community organizations. If you are comfortable asking those you know for some names, it can never hurt to give them a call and check out their recommendations. You may also wish to consult your phone book or use the Internet as long as the Internet sites are reputable and affiliated with recognized professional groups. We recommend the website of the American Medical Association (www.assn.org) to help you locate a child and adolescent psychiatrist and the website of the American Psychological Association (www.apa.org) to find a child and adolescent psychologist. You may also wish to contact your family doctor or a public health nurse who could recommend a mental health professional. Additionally, a crisis line, especially one for teens, or any major mental health center in your area, should be able to provide names of individuals and services to meet your teen's and family's needs.

You may personally know a child and adolescent mental health professional who could give you ideas about services for you and/or your teen. You may be tempted to ask this professional to see your child. We strongly advise against this for several reasons. First, it often becomes awkward for you, your teen, and the professional to respect the need for privacy and confidentiality. You may want to get more details about your teen's therapy, and, because you know the professional, feel more comfortable asking for it. The professional may want to share more details than she might otherwise do since she knows you. As a result, your teen may hesitate to share his feelings with the professional because he fears she may tell you or judge him. Maintaining professional boundaries is important to the success of any therapy, and in these cases, there is more opportunity to break those rules, ending in dissatisfaction for all.

How Can I Prepare for the Assessment?

When you make the first call to the professional/agency, don't be shy about asking questions. You have every right to know the professional's qualifications, as well as the type of therapy that she provides. Ask her what the research says about her therapy approach. Ask if she provides both assessment and treatment. You may wish to know how long therapy typically lasts. You should feel comfortable that your questions are answered. If you ask about wait lists, don't be surprised if the wait list is over six months for a first-time assessment. Wait lists can be long, and if you ever feel that your teen is deteriorating or needs immediate assistance, don't hesitate to take him to the Emergency Room of your local hospital.

> **Common Questions Parents Ask**
>
> - Can you help us?
> - Is my child's problem treatable?
> - What is the diagnosis?
> - Do we need more testing?
> - Should my child get treatment?
> - Is it my fault?
> - Should I get treatment?
> - What are your recommendations?
> - How long is treatment and how much will it cost?
> - Can you recommend some books to read?
> - What happens next?
> - What is your cancellation policy?

Often parents worry that they will be judged by professionals when they seek help for mental health issues. Mental health care professionals are there to support families, not judge and blame them. They are there to help design a treatment plan that takes all the pieces into consideration. Teens and parents should feel comfortable asking questions. We hear many kinds of questions from parents and teens, such as those listed in the sidebar at left.

No question is silly. If your mental health professional does not ask you if you have questions, don't be shy about sharing your list with her! If the therapist tells you that she does a "different type" of therapy, or that it takes a long time before you will see progress, or that it is a new therapy that no one in the area offers, get more information! These are red flags! And always ask for explanations if you do not understand something.

What Does a Psychiatric/Mental Health Assessment Consist of?

A psychiatric or mental health assessment is essentially a conversation or interview taking place between the professional, the parent(s), the teenager, and possibly other family members. It usually consists of a set of questions aimed to help the professional better understand the problem so that a diagnosis and recommendations for treatment can be made.

Each assessment varies according to the professional's style and preference. Sometimes, it consists of an interview with the child, an interview with the parent(s), and sometimes a family interview as well. A comprehensive assessment will last on average for two to three hours and may take place over one or more office visits. Sometimes information is collected with parent(s) and teen together. Depending on the age and level of maturity of your teen, more may be collected from you than from the adolescent himself. However, professionals often will interview teens on their own.

An individual interview with the child provides the opportunity for him to freely share thoughts and feelings about his life, his relationships at home and at school, and any other issues in a confidential manner. We encourage individual time with teens, as it helps them express concerns that they may feel uncomfortable sharing with their parent(s) present. In addition, it gives the teen a message that his individual perspective is valued and respected. It may promote a positive therapeutic alliance between the teen and the professional. When the presenting concern is related to depression, it is also likely that the professional will ask questions about suicidal thoughts and suicidal behavior. Asking about suicide does not "put ideas into the child's head," but rather provides assurance to him that people care for him. It gives the child the opportunity to talk about it, if in fact he has contemplated it.

In general, during the interview with the parent and teen, or with each alone, the professional will get a detailed picture about:

- the current concerns and stresses at home, at school, and in the community,
- the history of the problem,
- the child's development, health, illness and treatments, and medication,
- family relationships,
- school and friends,
- parent and family medical/psychiatric history.

If needed, laboratory studies such as blood tests, x-rays, or special assessments (for example, psychological, educational, speech and language evaluation) will be obtained during the assessment.

You and your teen may also be asked to complete questionnaires that further contribute to the assessment. We use a set of questionnaires that have proven to be accurate in determining the intensity and severity of the depression. Some examples include: the Children's Depression Inventory (CDI) (Kovacs, 1983) and the Beck Depression Inventory (BDI) (Beck, 1961), which has been revised and updated over the years. Questionnaires designed to determine whether another condition such as AD/HD or anxiety is present may also be used.

In addition, it is not uncommon for the professional to ask parents (and the teen) for permission to obtain information from significant others (school teachers, counselors, specialists, other relatives). Any consent requesting information is signed by the parent and also the teen, if he is of legal age to give his own informed medical consent. (In most states, this age is eighteen, but it is younger in a few states and older in a few states; in Canada it is sixteen.) Even if your teen is not of legal age, it is a good idea to include him in signing consents, as it demonstrates respect for him and may help to engage him in the assessment and treatment process.

Following the interviews, the professional arrives at a diagnosis and recommendations, which are shared with the teen and family. A treatment plan, which considers all the information from the interviews and questionnaires, is developed and shared with you. If you are not comfortable with the recommendations, feel free to ask questions and raise your concerns. It is important to discuss any hesitations you have about the recommendations. It is more important to identify obstacles in the treatment plan at the outset than to go along with something that you don't believe will work.

A Word about Confidentiality

In general, the mental health professional will not divulge what your teen confides in him or her, either during assessment or treatment. This shows respect for your teen's emerging autonomy, and builds trust in the relationship between teen and professional.

Although therapists need to respect confidentiality, they have an ethical and legal responsibility to tell you if there are any concerns about the safety of your teen or the safety of others. If the professional determines that your child has been or is experiencing suicidal thoughts and/or behavior, this information would be shared with you and a clear plan would be developed to prevent any suicidal gestures.

What Conditions Need to Be Ruled Out?

There are other conditions besides depression that sometimes produce symptoms such as grief, adjustment reactions, and trauma. These conditions can mimic depression and were discussed in Chapter 1. As they occur in response to specific events your teen reports, these conditions can generally be ruled out by a physician examining your teen. However, there are other psychiatric disorders that can show symptoms similar to depression which need to be considered by the mental health professional you consult. For example, anxiety disorders can be associated with depressed mood, particularly if they have persisted untreated for several years. The social isolation resulting from social phobia, for example, can look like social withdrawal associated with depression. Similarly, Oppositional Defiant Disorder (a condition in which the child or teen consistently refuses to cooperate with authority, to the point where it interferes with important daily activities) can mimic the negativity and irritability characteristic of teen depression. Unlike major depression, however, both of these conditions tend to persist for years, and do not change dramatically from month to month.

Teens who consume alcohol or illicit drugs can also appear depressed or withdrawn, either from drug withdrawal or from attempts to hide their habit. If you suspect this possibility, look into it, even if it means breeching your teen's privacy. The risks associated with drugs are often even greater than those associated with depression. When in doubt, check with a professional. Many teens suffer from more than one problem, and it can't hurt to have a thorough diagnostic assessment.

What Happens After the Assessment and During Treatment?

Following the assessment, certain recommendations will be made that could range from reading some books such as this one, to having regular weekly therapy sessions, to taking medication. Treatment will depend on your teen's specific presenting concerns. The professional(s) who conducts the initial assessment may or may not be the professional who provides the treatment. In our clinic, following the initial assessment, we often refer a teen for therapy to another qualified professional on our team who can see the teen for about twelve to fifteen sessions on a regular basis over a three- to four-month period. If the teen is not put on medication at the time of the assessment but that option was discussed as a future possibility, the therapist will monitor progress carefully and reassess the need for medication with the teen, family, and psychiatrist in a couple of months.

It is important to ask about your role in therapy. Sometimes parents are involved in some of the sessions to help provide information about progress at home and at school. Therapists may offer parents ideas about ways they could further help their teen at home as well. Do communicate with the therapist regularly, but also respect the boundaries between your teen and his therapist. You may want to know every detail of what is going on, but this does not respect your teen's growing need for privacy. It also puts the therapist in an awkward position, since he or she must reassure the teen that confidentiality will be respected. Trust that your teen is addressing his issues with the therapist. On the other hand, it is a good idea to clarify at the outset of therapy how often you can expect an update on the progress being made in therapy. This usually consists of a brief synopsis of progress in terms of goals and achievements, as well as areas where more work is needed and how you can help.

If you don't see any progress after several months, discuss this with the professional and with your teen and ask what progress they have observed. It may be that changes are happening, but they are not observable in your teen's behavior at home. Alternatively, if nobody is observing change, this is a good opportunity to problem-solve about how to overcome obstacles to change.

What If My Teen Refuses Therapy?

Once your teen is assessed by a mental health professional, it still doesn't guarantee participation in treatment. Many teens balk at participating in an activity that, in their view, is their parents' idea. See if you can contract with your child to "give it a try" and decide on how many sessions will constitute a reasonable "try."

We usually suggest an initial four- or five-session contract, if possible. A contract is a simple agreement that you make with your teen that he will agree to go to the appointment. You could say, *"Let's give it a fair try so we don't give up too soon. You could go five times and then at the end of the fifth session, we can talk about what is going well and what is not going well. We will only be able to know if it helps by giving it a good try."* By the fourth or fifth session, the teen will often find his own reasons for continuing. If not, he may not be ready for treatment at that point. You can still use the ideas in this book, monitor your teen's progress, and use emergency services if he deteriorates. Occasionally, a different therapist has better luck, but (in general) don't let your teen "fire" more than one. If two therapists are deemed unsuitable, it's more likely your teen's issue than the therapist's. Don't despair. Many teens are not ready for treatment on the first try, but can benefit from it later.

Key Points

1. Make a list of the symptoms that your teen is experiencing that are concerning you.
2. If you feel your teen could benefit from a mental health assessment, talk to him about the idea of talking to a professional.
3. Explore various ways to locate a professional who can help. Ask people you trust about services or about child and adolescent specialists in your area
4. Make a list of questions that you would ask a professional about herself and her services.
5. If you decide your teen should see a professional, then this week, create a plan for approaching your teen about agreeing to see a mental health professional.
   - ✓ Make a list (with your teen) of qualities of a therapist that are important to him (you may want to consider gender, time of appointment, office location, fees, etc.)
   - ✓ Think about creative ways that you would handle resistance from your teen about pursing an assessment.
   - ✓ If your teen continues to refuse the idea, set an appointment up for yourself to talk to a professional about your concerns.
   - ✓ In the midst of your search, don't forget to look for the positives and the things that are going right with your teen!

What is Normal for Adolescents?

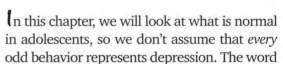

In this chapter, we will look at what is normal in adolescents, so we don't assume that *every* odd behavior represents depression. The word "normal" when talking about adolescence can be somewhat of a contradiction, insofar as there are many variations on what is considered "normal" at this stage of life. So, it becomes important to sift out behaviors that may be "odd," mildly moody, and transient but still "normal," versus behaviors that border on or indicate depressive symptoms.

Barb: *Barb was a sweet, pixie-faced girl with auburn hair and an interest in literature. The week after turning fourteen, she dyed her hair jet black and had her tongue*

Progress Check

How many "small positives" were you able to identify in your teen this past week? Were you surprised at how many there are, when you really pay attention to them? Encouraging those positives is one of the most helpful things parents can do, so it's great that you are becoming more aware of them!

If it applies to you, how did it go with talking to your teen about pursuing an outside opinion for some help?

pierced. Her clothes soon matched the "new look." She joined the underground "anarchist club" at school, and her taste in music changed. Shocked as she was, her mother tried to approach the changes with humor, without being unduly critical. "How's the graveyard gang?" she inquired when Barb's new friends hid as she approached. "Give them my regards." "I will, Mom," Barb replied with a smile.

Some things had changed, but many had stayed the same. Barb continued to write for the school newspaper, albeit with a greater social conscience. Her grades, though not at the top of the class, continued to be good. She kept in regular contact with her best friend, even though the friend did not share her new interests. She continued to take care of the family dog. She told her mother when she thought she might be out later than usual, and even asked her for advice occasionally. Barb's appearance had changed dramatically, but her basic personality had not.

She eventually decided to become a journalist, where she felt her writing talent could be used to inform others and "make a difference."

As part of her adolescent quest for identity, Barb tried on new styles and new ideas. Importantly, however, she maintained the key relationships in her life and continued to behave in a responsible manner in most areas. She modified her goals as a result of considering new ideas, but didn't fundamentally change them. Thus, Barb's dramatic-looking changes could be considered within the normal range. Given the odd peer group, her family might want to keep an eye on Barb for any signs of deterioration, but her ongoing, good communication with her mother should be helpful in this regard.

What Is Normal in Adolescence?

In the past, people thought that adolescence was a time of dramatic emotional turmoil. Recent studies, however, have shown that this is not the case, as 80 percent of teens get through adolescence with minimal or no psychiatric problems. Nevertheless, 20 percent of teens do experience some form of psychiatric disturbance during their adolescent years. Thus, your depressed teen is certainly not alone in her suffering. Besides depression, other symptoms considered "abnormal" include:

- antisocial behavior (for example, illegal activities),
- suicidal statements (including groups of teens who may jointly make suicide "pacts"),
- significant deterioration of school performance, or
- significant anxiety that interferes with day-to-day activities.

These behaviors are considered out of the range of normal and are red flags that need psychiatric attention. If your child falls into this category, get help.

Although adolescence is not necessarily a time of great turmoil, it *is* a time of great changes—physically, emotionally, mentally, and behaviorally. The changes most adolescents must cope with are discussed below.

Physical Changes

Pubertal development occurs in early adolescence, and with it comes increased self-consciousness in many teens, and some increased need for self-care (for example, using deodorants). There are some gender-specific advantages and disadvantages for adolescents whose bodies mature earlier. Boys who mature earlier have an advantage socially, as their greater size and strength are respected by peers. Girls who mature later have an advantage academically, as they are less distracted by male attention than their early-maturing peers. Whatever the rate of maturation in your teen, try to be sensitive to his or her increased need for privacy and potential embarrassment about physical development. Be positive about growing up and becoming a young man or young woman.

Mental Changes

Until the age of eleven or twelve, children are concrete thinkers. They see things in black and white and have less ability to see the "gray" areas. For example, a concrete thinker who receives a desired phone call from a friend may assume she is liked and popular. Likewise, if she does not receive a desired call from a friend, she assumes the friend does not like her. Hypothetical and futuristic thinking is not a part of concrete thinking.

Abstract reasoning (beginning around age thirteen in most children) allows for speculations and hypotheses about different possibilities, and some increased ability to plan ahead and "look before you leap." Unfortunately, it also allows for more worries and existential concerns (for example, questions about the purpose of one's life, or the nature of the universe or God). In depressed teens, this type of reasoning can lead to unhealthy, prolonged rumination (reviewing the same thought or worry or scenario repeatedly). A depressed teen may think, "I am totally unpopular. No one will ever like me." All teens reflect on their place in the world occasionally, but such negative thinking, especially when left untreated, can become habitual and actually perpetuate further depression.

It's not unusual for teens to challenge familiar and family beliefs at this age. Another "side effect" of abstract reasoning is the ability to argue more effectively. As they come to realize that you are not perfect, teens will identify your faults more readily. Don't take it personally. Set limits when needed. For example, you may wish to say to your teen, "It is OK to express your feelings but it is not OK to yell or scream or swear at me." Remember, for some teens arguing is just a way of exercising the brain.

Another notable change in thinking is that most teens become more able to be organized and goal directed as their brain matures. This may be more evident at school, where they are required to organize their thoughts in essays and open-ended test questions. Essentially, their brains are becoming more sophisticated as they prepare for adulthood.

Emotional Changes

Beginning in the 1950s, psychologist Erik Erikson described a series of stages and challenges that each individual passes through in their emotional development. In teens, he termed the main challenge "Identity versus Role Diffusion." This is the time when the teen is challenged to ask, "Who am I?" By exploring this question, the teen is establishing an identity that is clear and distinct from the expectations of others. This process includes gradually developing independence from one's family of origin. A teen who successfully meets this challenge will come out of it with a strong sense of identity and clear goals for the future.

Erikson termed the main challenge of the pre-teen years (ages six to twelve) "Industry versus Inferiority," reflecting the need for recognition for one's accomplishments at this age. In the late teen and early adult years, he termed the main emotional challenge "Intimacy versus Isolation," reflecting the struggle to establish and maintain healthy, close relationships.

Erikson referred to these challenges as "stages," but we now know that there is a great deal of overlap among them, and people who do not resolve a particular challenge at one age may return to it later. Thus, adolescents who are still working on "industry" haven't necessarily missed the boat on "identity" and vice versa. For example, a teen who is focused on "industry" may be struggling with feelings of competency. She may be investing more energy into academic activities and expending less energy on self-reflection. Her thinking may be more noticeably concrete as she works to acquire a sense of achievement in school or to master other intellectual activities. A teen focused on "identity" may be less focused on school and more on finding a peer group that shares her values. However, all adolescents face these challenges to a greater or lesser degree.

Behavioral Changes

Identity progresses from establishing yourself as separate from your parents, to finding a group, special activity, or mentor to identify with or idealize, to then finding and accepting your individual identity, warts and all. Because this process takes years, young adolescents often get stuck between wanting to do things independently versus wanting their parents' support. (For example, "My mother won't let me go there" is often used to resist peer pressure, even if it's the teen herself who doesn't want to go there!)

The desire for independence also waxes and wanes depending on circumstances. A teen may look very independent one day, and need a great deal of support the next. Try to accept a certain amount of inconsistency with humor, but be clear what the rules are about important behaviors (for example, attending school, coming home by a certain time, and issues related to safety). Teens need to have a say, but parents must still do what's in their best interest. Freedoms should depend on the level of responsibility the teen has demonstrated. Don't expect teens to acknowledge your advice, though. They often appear not to listen even though they are (it's not cool to admit your parents are right).

Heightened self-consciousness means "all the world's a stage" for teenagers, and the audience of their peers becomes very (sometimes overly) important. Young adolescents also tend to form highly exclusive groups or cliques, leaving some feeling alienated. Older adolescents become gradually more accepting of individual differences, usually forming more inclusive social groups toward the end of high school. Until then, kids who are not part of the "popular group" often have to focus on a few peers with a common interest (difficult for some).

Encourage your teen to treasure the friends she does have, rather than yearning for those who won't accept her. Also, foster tolerance by encouraging your teen to be respectful, interested, and open to learning from a variety of people with different appearances, aptitudes, and orientations—whether your child is part of the "in" group or not. This attitude makes for healthier high school environments, and probably wouldn't be a bad thing for the rest of society either.

> **What Other Parents Have Said**
>
> - "Everything's more intense. He went from being a pony to a wild stallion."
> - "I can't *make* her do things anymore. I have to redirect her energy. It's like jujitsu."
> - "He really pushes my buttons. I have to let my husband handle some of the 'hot spots.'"
> - "I keep having to remind myself she's not me."

Dealing with Normal Teen Behavior

For parents, adolescent development can challenge our ability to deal with strong emotions, and even affect our perception of ourselves (especially if we had difficulty with adolescence ourselves). Furthermore, parents often feel they have less influence over the behavior of adolescents than of younger children. Handling your teen's behavior may be especially problematic if she seems to be deliberately "pushing your buttons"—that is, reacting in ways that predictably make you upset.

When You Feel a "Button Being Pushed"

Many times, your teen's responses are less deliberate than they first appear to be. Think about these possibilities to understand underlying reasons you feel as if your buttons are being pushed:

- Maybe the teen's behavior reminds you of someone who hurt you in the past.
- Maybe her behavior elicits reactions from you that are like those of someone who hurt you in the past.

In both situations, a negative relationship from the past seems to be "replayed" between you and your teen. Also consider the following possibilities, which are more relevant to your own identity development:

- Maybe the teen's behavior reminds you of an undeveloped part of yourself. (For example, you may pride yourself in being strong and

self-reliant, but your teen is repeatedly asking for help with the smallest thing—perhaps you envy her ability to rely on others.)
- Maybe the teen's behavior reminds you of a part of yourself you dislike.
- Maybe the teen's behavior reminds you of something you missed out on in your own adolescence (For example, your teen confidently speaks her mind, even when it annoys you, while you were too considerate of others' feelings to be so bold.)
- Maybe you miss being the mother or father of a child, and are irritated by reminders of the fact that she is now an adolescent. (For example, you are upset that your adolescent now does things alone or with others that you used to do with her.)

Consider whether one of the above may be intensifying your feelings about the situation. Then, give yourself a chance to calm down, separate your own feelings from those of your teen, and try to put yourself in her shoes. An empathic parental response should be easier in this frame of mind.

Dealing with Teen Behavior

Here are some parents' ideas for handling teen behavior, regardless of whether the teen has a diagnosis.
- Don't take it personally.
- Don't expect respect, but give it.
- Don't punish endlessly.
- Support independence by letting your teen do some things for herself. (For example, don't argue about why you won't get her a Popsicle from the fridge; just don't do it.)
- If your teen won't go to her room for a time out: give her space, send her to the store, go to your own room, or have an immediate consequence.
- Give her choices, but with limits. (For example, "Do you want to do your math first or your history?"—implying that some sort of homework will be done, but you're willing to negotiate on the order of subjects. Or, "Would you like to take the bus to school or walk?"—implying that school attendance is compulsory, but mode · of transportation is negotiable.)

Factors Linked to Resilience (Better Outcomes) in Teens

Recently in attempts to better understand mental illness, mental health professionals have identified certain factors that help protect individuals from illness such as depression. Resilience factors, or things that help people stay healthy in the presence of risk factors (Kaufman, 2000), *may* prevent a depressive episode from occurring or prevent depression from getting worse. Resilience has been defined as the "ability to persevere and adapt when things go awry" (Reivich, K. & Shatte, A., 2002). However, if resilience is offset by substantial risk factors (for example, a strong family history of depression), your teen may still get depressed. On the positive side, though, resilience factors can improve coping and recovery from the illness. They may even reduce the risk of recurrence. Therefore, they are still important to keep in mind, and to enhance if possible. Research has identified the following as resilient factors for depression

- Feeling cared for by at least one other person;
- Parents get along reasonably well and are relatively consistent in relation to how they deal with the teen (expectations and limits set by each parent are similar);
- Adults model a positive perspective on situations;
- Social connections (i.e., the teen has friends);
- The opportunity to learn from life sometimes;
- A coherent system of values/meaning;
- Temperamental "fit" with the family is reasonable (for example, a highly athletic teen may feel out of place in a family of sedentary academics, and vice versa);
- Routines and clear rules at home;
- Authoritative parenting (basically, setting clear limits but in a thoughtful way that takes the child's feelings and developmental needs into account, providing explanations when needed, and allowing more input from the child with greater maturity).

Conclusion

This chapter offered a very brief overview of normal development in adolescence to help parents sift out those behaviors that are typical of this age group from those that seem to border on, or be within, the spectrum of depression. If you are not sure whether your teen is behaving normally, we advise further reading or research on the topic and professional consultation. Also, bear in mind that even depressed teens show a range of behaviors where some are typical and others are not. We encourage you to review and try the strategies described in this chapter as you try to understand your teen's needs. If more help is needed and your strategies for managing problematic behavior do not seem to be working, seek some advice from professionals.

Exercise: What's Hard about Parenting Normal Teens?

1. Think about the two or three difficult behaviors you can identify in your teen.
2. Compare your teen to others of similar age.
3. Think which of the difficulties are:
    a. problems likely related to depression,
    b. problems unlikely to be related to depression,
    c. probably part of normal adolescence.
4. Think about any problematic behavior that you concluded was "normal." What would be a good way to deal with this behavior? (Feel free to look back at the chapter if it helps). Try it out this week.

Key Points

80% of adolescents do not suffer significant emotional or behavioral problems. 20% do have such problems. Here are a few examples contrasting the 80% in the "normal" group and the 20% who have more serious problems:

- Not wanting to talk to parents at times is normal during the teen years.
- Not wanting to talk to anyone, including peers, is not.

- Sometimes coming home later than your curfew may be a normal expression of the adolescent desire for autonomy.
- Not coming home all night is not normal.

- Wondering out loud why people commit suicide is a normal existential question.
- Saying, with conviction, that you'd rather be dead is not.

- A temporary drop in grades when adjusting to a new school is normal.
- Failing a grade is not.

- Being anxious about what your peers think of you is normal.
- Being so anxious that you can't look people in the eye is not.

II

The
L.E.A.P.
Approach

L.E.A.P.

A Problem-Solving Approach

To achieve the goals of the book, we focus on employing a problem-solving approach. We do this because we see parents as key participants in discovering *solutions* to children's depression and depression-related problems. After all, who knows your son or daughter better than you do? The approach described here is *central* to all topics addressed in the remainder of the book, and thus, it is essential to read this chapter first in order to apply the information in the following chapters to your lives. The L.E.A.P. approach will provide a useful, step-by-step process for you to implement and experiment with new ideas.

The L.E.A.P. Approach

The L.E.A.P. approach is based on principles of cognitive-behavioral therapy (CBT). Essentially, CBT involves recognizing and reflecting on persistent negative or depressing thoughts that lead to negative feelings and behaviors. Then, CBT allows people to replace them with more useful, positive, and realistic ones using a variety of strategies.

Studies have shown that CBT is one of the most effective types of therapy for adolescents and adults experiencing depression. Initially developed by Dr. Aaron Beck, CBT has been widely used for over thirty years by many mental health professionals across North America and Europe to treat depression. Like other psychotherapies, it is based on talking, but the focus of the talking is on current problems and active problem-solving. The therapist works with the teen to identify specific situations in which he felt unhappy. Then, the negative thoughts and behaviors associated with this situation are examined, and alternative ways of thinking and behaving are explored. The teen is encouraged to test out these alternatives between sessions, to determine whether his negative feelings change as a result.

If your teen is seeing someone who practices CBT, your use of this book will be very complementary to the therapist's approach. However, it is not necessary that your teen's therapist be a CBT therapist in order for you and your teen to benefit from applying the L.E.A.P. approach as outlined in this book.

Traditionally and still today, a CBT approach often involves one person working with the therapist without assistance from other family members. However, since CBT has become the gold standard for treating depression, and particularly, since the approach has been applied to younger people, adaptations have been developed that include considerable parental involvement in treatment, as well as group treatments. What makes this book unique is that it offers you, the parent, an approach based on CBT principles that you may apply (without a therapist) to understand your feelings and create individually tailored problem-solving plans to benefit yourself and your teen.

Our L.E.A.P. approach is also based on circular thinking. When engaging in problem solving with your teen, you will be encouraged to map out your interactions with him. We encourage parents to "think circles, not lines." In other words, think about how your teen affects you *and* how you affect your teen, instead of just how your teen affects you *or* just how you affect your teen. Circular thinking implies a focus on relationships between people and paves the way for creative problem solving. We find there is less blaming of one person and more understanding between parents and teens when parents are able to view problems from a circular perspective.

The four-step L.E.A.P. approach can be summarized by the following acronym:

L:

Label and understand *my* own thoughts and emotions and begin to explore their influence on my behavior.

E:

Empathize with my teen for what he/she may be experiencing and **explore** ways to respond to him or her from an empathic perspective.

A:

Apply one alternative way to respond (either an attitude or an action or some of both) this week.

P:

Pick a follow-up time to evaluate the result, and **plan** ahead with everyone involved (other family members, school, professionals) about where to go from here.

You may notice that there are actually two "E" words in the "E" part of the L.E.A.P. plan, one that stands for "empathy" and one that stands for "explore ways to respond to the teen." Likewise, there are two "P" words in the "P" part— one for "pick a follow-up time" and one for "plan ahead." We chose to shorten the acronym to L.E.A.P. instead of L.E.E.A.P.P., but we do encourage you to remember all components of each of the L.E.A.P. words.

To begin a L.E.A.P. plan, you think about one particular problem that you would like to work on. You may want to fix all the problems at once or you may feel that you want to fix the depression itself. However, for L.E.A.P. plans to be successful, you must choose one situation or pattern of interaction that you'd like to see change. For example, you may wish to see your teen improve his hygiene or get up earlier. You may wish to help him become more active or less socially isolated. We encourage you to work on one situation at a time. There will be plenty of opportunity throughout the book to cover different situations. In fact, from Chapter 6 onward, you will be asked to do a L.E.A.P. plan based on each chapter's topic. We also think it is wise not to start with the most difficult problem first. It can be more rewarding to start small and see some progress than to take on the big stuff and feel disappointed if change doesn't occur.

If you are the type of parent who usually talks a lot to your teen about trying new things, you may want to try the L.E.A.P. approach unbeknownst to him and just see how things unfold when *you* try different strategies. On the other hand, if you feel a more collaborative approach is needed with your teen and with a particular problem, you may wish to enlist his help as you develop and implement the L.E.A.P. plan. In general, there are no hard and fast rules about involving your teen in making and applying the L.E.A.P. plan, except not to argue about it. Trust your past experience with your teen: Is he more receptive to talking? Or do "actions speak louder than words" for your teen?

Labeling Thoughts and Emotions

One of the most difficult, yet important steps of the L.E.A.P. approach is the first one: learning how to label your *own* thoughts and emotions. We don't mean examining thoughts and feelings about your teen's depression in general. We mean taking a moment to examine thoughts and feelings about the one situation you have chosen to work on. It is difficult because in the face of high intensity emotion from a teenager, we often don't take time to really reflect on our own thoughts and emotional states. However, if we don't identify and label the thoughts and emotions we are having about the situation, we end up repeating the same old behaviors ourselves and not moving ahead. Without self-reflection, change is not likely to occur because we do not allow ourselves to stop and really think about how we think, feel, and subsequently behave. However, once we identify and label our thoughts and related emotions, we become better equipped to effectively resolve issues.

In families, parents can influence their children by carefully examining their thoughts, feelings, and behaviors. Children, in turn, can learn by their parents' examples.

We have listed some questions below to help you reflect on this first important step in identifying your feelings (1-5) and thoughts (6-10) as you witness or experience the problematic situations that you will include in your L.E.A.P. plans as you progress through the book:

1. *How am I feeling right now as I am engaged in this conversation with my teen?* This is a good question to think of at the time that the problematic situation is unfolding. For example, if you are going to develop a L.E.A.P. plan related to your son's refusal to socialize, you ask yourself this question as soon as you witness the problematic behavior. Perhaps you witness him refusing to return a friend's phone call. Maybe you feel mad or frustrated, or maybe it makes you feel sorry for him or that things are hopeless and will never change. Whatever your feeling is, note it. It is important to notice so you can understand yourself and your behavior toward your teen.

2. *When I see my teen doing x, what do I feel?*

3. *What buttons get pushed when I hear my teen's concerns/complaints?* (i.e., what reactions are based on my own past experiences?) For example, one parent told us that her son was always making demands of her. Often when he was in the living room on the couch, he would tell her to get him a snack. She would be angry at his demands but would automatically do it. When she realized that his demands reminded her of how her father made similar demands on her mother, she realized that she was simply repeating her mother's passive behavior, which reinforced her father's disrespectful behavior. She realized these buttons from her childhood were being pushed by her son and was able to break the pattern by telling her son where the snacks were and that he was welcome to help himself.

4. *If I could pick one word that best describes my emotional state right now, what would it be?* This question is similar to the first one, where you check in on how you feel at the time the problematic situation is occurring.

5. *If I were to think about this problematic situation differently, how would my emotional reaction change?* For example, one mother believed that her son's negative thoughts about school would never change. The more she thought that way, the more hopeless she felt. When she agreed to notice times that there was any small step forward (e.g., he made a passing comment implying that the teacher cared about him), his mother noticed that her own thoughts were more positive and her emotions not so hopeless.

6. *What is going on in my own mind right now?* Again, this question helps you to identify your thoughts right at the time of the problematic situation.

7. *How am I making sense of this?* In other words, when you experience the problem, how do you understand or explain it? Some-

times getting a better sense of our beliefs about the root of a problem puts us in touch with how we respond to it. One father, who was a doctor and stressed good nutrition, believed that his daughter's refusal to eat was her way to intentionally push his buttons. By better understanding and challenging his beliefs about the cause of his daughter's behavior, he was more open to entertaining other reasons why she might not be eating.

8. *What thoughts seem to be constraining me from creative problem solving?* Depressive behaviors from teens have a way of inviting depressing thoughts in parents. Often it can take a lot of energy to stay positive and realistic in the face of the teen's depression. Thus, it is important to note the thoughts that might be constraining creative problem solving. Some examples include: "This will never change"; "There is little that I can do to help"; or "He is just like his father." When these thoughts predominate, the creative juices slow down.

9. *If there was one thought I could change about this situation/problem right now, what would it be?*

10. *If I did change my thinking about this situation, what difference might it make to my response?*

Below is a beginning list of some common negative emotional responses. Think of others as well and add to this list. The more you can generate, the more elaborate a list you can choose from when you focus on labeling your emotions for each particular problematic situation.

- Worry
- Sadness
- Anger
- Frustration
- Helplessness
- Fear
- Guilt
- Embarrassment
- Annoyance
- Irritation
- Impatience

Remember that all of these emotions are normal for all of us to feel once in a while. Parents of depressed teens may feel them more frequently and more intensely. You shouldn't feel bad about having these emotions. After all, you are dealing with very difficult situations. You care very much for your child and want to make things better for him. Therefore, when you see things slide, it is not unusual to feel discouraged. Even if you think your emotions are not good emotions for a parent to feel about his or her child, you need to be honest about how you feel in order for the L.E.A.P. approach to work.

Finally, it is important to reflect on how your own behavior may affect your teen. It may be that you inadvertently choose words or actions that push your teen's buttons! For example, a parent may say, "You can't pass if you don't go to school." While this may be true, the teen may feel that his parent is controlling him and dismissing his feelings. This comment is not likely to encourage him to make an effort to attend school. It is worthwhile to be a fly on the wall to your own behavior and notice what you say or do that may be perpetuating the problem. Remember, think circles, not lines!

Empathy and Exploring

The next step in the L.E.A.P. plan is to feel empathy toward your teen in the situation at hand and then to explore ways to respond to him in the particular situation from an empathic perspective.

The term "empathy" is often misunderstood, so it warrants a bit of explanation. Empathy is an accurate understanding of another person's emotional experience. It does not mean being sucked into feeling exactly how the other person is feeling (that's called "sympathy"), nor does it mean being nice all the time. For example, you can empathize with an isolated, withdrawn teen about how difficult it is to get to school but at the same time give him a supportive, but firm push out the bedroom door. The latter is "empathy in action" because it is what he needs to get better.

To be empathic, you must be able to clearly tell the difference between your own feelings and your teen's feelings about a situation. Then, put yourself in his shoes. Usually, this leads to an understanding of how he is feeling. However, don't assume you know the feeling! You may be missing information about the situation and may need to explore in more detail before sharing your observations. For example, if a peer makes a comment about your teen that sounds rude, you may think that your teen is feeling hurt or embarrassed. It's possible, though, that the apparently rude comment is a current slang expression that represents a compliment. (The word "bad," for example, in some circles actually means good!) If you're not sure you understand your teen's feelings about a given situation, test it out. Try putting into words how you think he is feeling and see what happens. If you're being empathic, the teen will nod, tell you you're right, or at least not object to what you're saying. If you're off the mark, he will almost always let you know. Modify your idea and try again.

Empathizing with your teen is the one aspect of using the L.E.A.P. approach that is different from other problem-solving approaches. The reason we include this step is that depressed individuals may perceive their family members as uncaring and overly controlling (so-called "affectionless control"). In part, this may be due to the distortions associated with depressed thinking. We'll talk about those in detail in a later chapter. In part, it may be due to the difficulty families experience behaving in a caring and respectful manner toward a depressed teen who may appear irritable, passive, and uninterested in others much of the time. Regardless of where the teen's negative perception of others comes from, though, changing it is an important part of recovery from depression. Empathic responses are very helpful in this regard. Empathic responses also work better from a parent's point of view: teens are more likely to cooperate when they feel understood than when they feel bossed around or coerced.

The most important outcome of you showing empathy is for your teen to feel understood. It is not always necessary to voice your empathy in words. Often a nod or a look that gives an understanding message is all that a teen needs. In fact, if you find yourself trying to empathize with your teen and your teen is not responding, you may want to back off a bit and try again later. If he is rejecting your efforts, he is likely not experiencing your actions as empathy. He may be experiencing them as sympathy or may be finding your efforts intrusive. In any case, it will be clear if he is not responding. Don't take it personally; just try again later.

Some questions for reflection:

1. How might *I feel* if I thought all of my friends hated me?
2. If I felt anxious and worried about failing all the time, what might *I think* about myself?
3. What might *I do* if I believed that my parents were always on my case?

These are some of the feelings, thoughts, and actions that may occur in a depressed teen.

Applying Alternative Ideas

Once you have labeled your thoughts and emotions about a given problem related to your teen's depression and you have tried to empathize with him, it is time to try to actively implement new ways to manage that problem. We encourage parents to think of applying new ideas and new approaches in a spirit of experimentation. Think of an idea that you may have overlooked or dismissed in the past (or a new one you've just heard about) and experiment with applying it to a specific situation. Being so specific may sound discouraging to some parents. After all, they've encountered hundreds of difficult situations with their teens. How effective is it to dissect every single one? Fortunately, you are unlikely to end up doing hundreds of problem-solving exercises. After a half dozen or so, most parents begin to recognize some recurrent patterns and some constructive things they can do that apply to more than one situation. These constructive "gems" begin to produce noticeable change if used regularly for a month or two.

Research shows that it takes twelve to fifteen weeks to chip away at any old patterns and begin to shape new ones. Nevertheless, problems can only be solved one at a time. Try to be patient and don't give up too soon! Integrating new ideas and making changes takes time. Although we use the word "L.E.A.P.," we fully endorse baby steps one day at a time!

When thinking about experimentation with new ideas, consider the following:

- What have I done so far? What has worked well? (Don't throw out all the old approaches; some may work well if tried more consistently!)
- What are the pros and cons of trying this new idea? What can we gain? Lose? Make a list.

- How might my teen react to my idea/my new approach?
- What do you and your teen need to do to make this successful?
- What would success look like and how will you know you've succeeded?

Pick a Follow-Up Time and Plan Ahead

No plan is complete without detailed evaluation and follow-up. As the last step in the L.E.A.P. plan, it is critical to pick a follow-up time to evaluate the result. Typically, when activities become routine and are scheduled in, they happen. Thus, making an informal "appointment" with your teen and/or others involved to note progress is important. When change is gradual and slow, it becomes even more critical to note small successes along the way. All too often, ideas and new approaches are quickly dismissed, rejected, or discarded because they do not fully cure the problem. Yet, without careful consideration, you can easily miss that one aspect of the plan that went particularly well and made a difference, even a small but progressive one. Thus, regular, consistent evaluation can help everyone involved to see the light at the end of the tunnel. Noting progress also encourages families to plan ahead together. Some questions related to evaluation and planning ahead are:

- When should I/we check in with each other to see how it went? Set a time.
- What went well?
- What is the thing (even the smallest thing) that made the (positive) difference?
- What do we *not* want or need to change? Remember to conserve what is already going well!
- What still needs ongoing attention and work?
- What would happen if we discarded this idea now?
- What would happen if we altered it some or left it in place and kept moving forward?

Problem-Solving Tips

Successful problem-solving depends on thinking very specifically about situations in which your teen's behavior has been troubling or difficult to manage. Try to think of a recent example of a challenging situation within the last few days. What did your child say? What did you say? What did your child do? What did you do? Reconstruct the sequence of events in your mind as if they had been videotaped on a camcorder. Doing this often reveals at what point in the situation you could have chosen to think, feel, or do something differently that might have altered the process or the outcome, or at least how you felt about the process and/or the outcome.

When recalling events, try to avoid thinking in generalizations such as, "She's always so disrespectful," or, "He never does anything if I don't nag him." These state-

Who to Involve in L.E.A.P. Plans

For the most part, parents we have worked with have developed L.E.A.P. plans which include themselves and their teens only. And if the problem you're working on pertains only to an interaction between you and your teen, you may not wish or need to include others. However, depending on the problem situation that you have identified, you may need to consider including others in the plan. If the situation affects others at home or at school, who should be included? Careful thought needs to go into answering this question.

It is critically important to respect your teen's privacy and feelings. You may need to draw boundaries around certain L.E.A.P. plans. For example, your child may not want the whole family involved in helping him with his hygiene. On the other hand, he may have very supportive siblings who he would see as cheerleaders for him in his efforts to improve his hygiene. He may not want his teacher aware of his sensitivity to peer criticism. Then again, he may feel OK with you telling his teacher about his social problems and appreciate her quiet support of his efforts. If you think that expanding the number of people involved will help, try it out. But check with your teen about your plans to make sure he is on board and your efforts will not backfire.

ments are not only imprecise, but they are also likely to make you feel resentful and defeated, and therefore less motivated to help your teen. The more specific you can be, the more likely you are to generate new solutions to old problems.

Key Points

L.E.A.P. Means:

- **Label** and understand *my* own thoughts and emotions and begin to explore their influence on my behavior.

- **Empathize** with my teen for what he/she may be experiencing and **explore** ways to respond to him or her from an empathic perspective.

- **Apply** one way to respond differently (either an attitude or an action or some of both) this week.

- **Pick a follow-up time** to evaluate the result, and **plan ahead** with everyone involved (other family members, school, professionals) about where to go from here.

Although it may sound backwards, it's often helpful to start with the last step (Pick a Follow-Up Time) when first implementing this approach. Therefore, find a weekly time (ten or fifteen minutes) that you can devote to working on the L.E.A.P. approach consistently. Mark it on the calendar and make it a priority! When you have some time to sit down for fifteen minutes and think about a situation that is concerning you (start small!), we recommend you go through each step of the L.E.A.P. plan. Then decide when you would like to begin to implement it (it could be the same day or another). We recommend that you pick a follow-up time about one week from implementing the plan.

The L.E.A.P. Program in Action

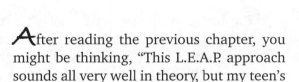

After reading the previous chapter, you might be thinking, "This L.E.A.P. approach sounds all very well in theory, but my teen's problems are complex. I don't see how merely empathizing with him and trying something new is going to change anything." This chapter will show you how the approach has worked in the past for parents facing common situations with depressed teens. The stories we present in this chapter are based on situations that parents have shared with us over the years and represent a variety of many teens' experiences. The names we use are purely fictional and do not represent a specific individual or family.

Greta and the Sour Milk

For the past few months, Mrs. Sampson has noticed that her daughter Greta, age fourteen, leaves spoiled food and garbage in her room. Yesterday, she found sour milk on the windowsill. On numerous occasions, she has asked Greta to clean up after herself, but Greta typically ignores her or tells her she will get to it after this or after that. Mrs. Sampson becomes very frustrated and angry, cannot understand how anyone can live with the smell of spoiled food, and finds herself shouting at Greta to "clean up her junk pile." In turn, Greta shouts back, "So what?" Then she slams the door to her room and stays in it for hours listening to the type of music that (to add fuel to the fire) Mrs. Sampson disapproves of.

How can Mrs. Sampson apply the L.E.A.P. approach to this situation?

L:

Label thoughts and emotions: "I *feel angry* and *embarrassed* that my child won't clean up after herself. I am *frustrated* and *disappointed* that Greta won't listen to me. When she says, "So what?" and slams the door, I *think* that she is behaving so irresponsibly and wonder if she will ever grow up! I find myself thinking that she is intentionally trying to get my goat! However, I am starting to see how these negative thoughts of mine only make it worse."

E:

Empathize: If I were in her shoes and feeling so low, maybe the last thing I would feel like doing is cleaning up too. I wonder if my yelling just reinforces her low feelings about herself? (But it is so hard for me not to yell when I'm angry!) However, I remember my own mother yelling at me at that age and it didn't help. She probably feels quite frustrated when I am on her case about this food problem. I'm sure other teenagers don't put their dishes away at times too, and "fessing up" when someone accuses you of doing something foolish isn't always easy.

Explore: Maybe I can ask her what makes cleaning up difficult for her? Maybe I can ask her how I can help? Maybe by talking *calmly* we can work out a way to help us both—to help her clean up the room and help me avoid yelling. One option might be to do a "room check" before going to school in the morning to help her remember. Staying calm but gently insisting that she wash out the mess might be another approach.

A:

Apply an alternative idea: One action that I am pleased with was that I did not make an issue of the music (even though it really bugs me!). That could have put us in a deeper rut. I know that I am unlikely to stay calm when I find flies swarming around the old food in her room, so maybe I'll just institute the room check, and be positive if she remembers to do it without reminders.

P:

Pick a follow up time: I'll see how it goes for a week, and then review it next Saturday.

Plan ahead: If it's still a problem, maybe I can get Bob (husband) to help.

Jebran and School Refusal

Jebran has been having great difficulty going to school. He says he is nervous about attending school and worries that peers will tease him as they have in the past. He often calls himself "useless" and stays in his room. Here is a L.E.A.P. plan completed by his mother.

L:

Label: My heart breaks (*sadness*) when I hear Jebran run himself down that way. I *feel sorry for him* and I wish I could keep him at home and nurse him until he's better. I wonder—did I cause this depression somehow? I ask myself that a lot and feel so *guilty*.

E:

Empathize: I may feel for Jebran and worry about him, but I can't let sympathy rule over empathy. Sympathy seems to stop me from giving him the help he needs. If I were empathetic, I would try and understand how it is for him but not let my own buttons get pushed and feel sorry for him. I might also recognize that what he says reflects his distorted, overly negative thoughts about himself. I may actually perpetuate those thoughts by allowing him to stay home! In the long run, he'll feel better if I don't let him wallow at home.

Explore: Rather than feel sorry for him, I need to notice his small, progressive steps. Maybe I can give him something to do when he starts to talk negatively, or ask him to help me with a chore. He's usually cooperative, so asking him to help me would create a nice opportunity to thank or praise him. This, in turn, may boost his confidence.

A:

Apply an alternative idea: I'll plan on at least one helpful thing for Jebran to do each day, unless he finds something he wants to do on his own.

P:

Pick a follow up time: I'll make note in a week's time if Jebran is doing more and wallowing less.
Plan ahead: Maybe I'll ask the teacher to give him a job to do in class as well.

Here is an example of a L.E.A.P. plan from Jebran's father:
L:
Label: I've given that boy every opportunity and every good thing I never had growing up. Now he just sits there like a bump on a log. It's *frustrating* to have a kid like that and it's *disgusting* that he can't get it together! No

matter what I do for him, it is never good enough. If I really sit back and think about it, I guess I feel *angry* and *helpless* and take it out on him.

E:

Empathize: The more I have learned about depression from professionals, the more I have come to realize that it is a legitimate illness. His illness reduces his energy level. No matter how many opportunities he's given, he has to have energy to pursue them. Taking it personally just makes me argumentative with Jebran. Empathizing with him might make him feel understood. Empathizing with him does not mean that I have to agree with his solutions!

Explore: Instead of feeling disgusted, maybe I can work on helping Jebran increase his energy level. I could go for a walk with him after work or throw a ball around. It might even help my blood pressure. Walking is probably better. I get too competitive when you put a baseball in my hand.

A:

Apply alternate plan: I'll plan to get home by 7:00 at the latest, so I can walk for half an hour with Jebran each day.

P:

Pick a follow up time: I'll give it two weeks and see what happens.

Plan ahead: If he's still not doing much, I'll talk to his doctor about maybe adjusting his medication.

Note that it's not unusual for parents of depressed teens (or all teens, for that matter) to have very different views of their offspring. Neither excessive sympathy (as Jebran's mother initially showed) nor a complete lack of empathy (as Jebran's father initially showed) is helpful. Both had to move away from these extreme positions to be able to answer the question, "What is best for Jebran?" L.E.A.P. plans are designed to help you answer that question, one situation at a time, for your teen.

If parents are both using the L.E.A.P. approach with the same teen, it is important that they consult each other regularly. Otherwise, one parent may unwittingly sabotage the other's plan, such as by planning a conflicting activity. Set aside at least ten or fifteen minutes once a week to decide what to do. Try to avoid criticizing each other's ideas or dismissing them before they have been tried. Be open to different possible solutions to problems, and see what works.

Allan and Indecision

Mr. and Mrs. Wong raised concerns that their fifteen-year-old son, Allan, has great difficulty making a decision about his weekend activities. Allan would pursue his dad about what they would do on the weekend. Mr. Wong would feel irritated and ask Allan what *he* wanted to do, which would only serve to invite Allan to pursue his father more. Mr. Wong developed a L.E.A.P. plan to help himself and his son in their vicious cycle of interaction.

L:

Label: I get so *irritated* when my son asks, "What are we doing this weekend?" like it's my responsibility to find him something to do! Why can't he just make up his mind? He is an intelligent kid. Surely he must have some interests of his own! (Perhaps Mr. Wong feels unfairly burdened, and he's clearly irritated and annoyed.)

E:

Empathize: I need to try and understand what is going on for Allan in order to break this cycle between us. I need to empathize with him. Maybe a reason for his indecision is that he is shy and doesn't have many friends to go out with, so it's hard for him to occupy himself on the weekends. Maybe he is not confident about his ability to make a decision (even seemingly simple ones), and worries he will make the wrong choice. Also, he always likes to know what's coming next, so maybe this is his way of reassuring himself about the plan for the weekend. Maybe his depression also makes it hard to find the energy to organize things for himself.

Explore: I could ask him what he wants to do, but he never has any ideas. I could give him choices, but he can't seem to make up his mind. I could also make the decision for him and see how he reacts, or give him a task to do to occupy himself. Maybe asking him to do something he doesn't like will prompt a decision about what he would *prefer* to do.

A:

Apply alternate plan: First, I could ask him to choose something. Then, if he can't decide in a few minutes, I'll let him know he's welcome to come along with me and do what I'm doing. (Note: Mr. Wong doesn't feel he has to go out of his way, decreasing his resentment, and a decision is made, decreasing his frustration.)

P:

Pick a follow up time: I'll see how this weekend goes, and on Sunday I'll decide whether I want to change anything next week.

Plan ahead: If it doesn't work, I won't throw away these ideas. I will try again next week. Maybe just asking him to choose something different will trigger a change in him, but I might not see it right away.

Dana and Picky Eating/Indecision

Mrs. Robertson is a single mom who enjoys taking her two children, Jessica and Dana, out to restaurants as a treat for everyone on Friday evenings. However, choosing a restaurant that suits Dana, age thirteen, is a real challenge. Whenever Mrs. Robertson asks which restaurant she wants to go to, Dana can't decide. She will suggest one and Dana will say, "That's no good." She makes another suggestion and that's no good either. Nothing is ever any good, until finally Mrs. Robertson just says, "Let's go here!" Dana is unhappy, and pouts and sulks all the way to the restaurant.

L:

Label: I feel *frustrated* with her always saying no to my ideas. She's so picky!

E:

Empathize: Maybe she is more picky than usual these days because depression is affecting her appetite. Maybe she can't accept a restaurant that isn't perfect, just like she can't accept herself unless she's perfect. (Perfectionism can be part of anxiety or depression.)

Explore: Maybe this is her way of keeping me paying attention to her instead of her sister, because she believes that I have a closer relationship with her sister. Maybe this is what underpins this negative cycle we get into. I also wonder if planning some time alone with her would help.

A:

Apply alternate plan: I should probably model decision making for her. On alternative weeks, each child will get a chance to pick the restaurant she wants. I know that Jessica will make up her mind easily. If Dana can't decide when it is her turn, I could offer a few choices (instead of dragging it out and getting into a conflict). If there is no decision by a set time, I will state to Dana that I will decide. Instead of allowing Dana to pine on it, I will try to use distraction and spend some quality time talking about other things in her life over dinner. If she continues to mope about the restaurant choice, I may need to set limits on going out for dinner on Fridays.

P:

Pick a follow up time: I am going to see how this goes for the next three Fridays and note any changes over time.

Plan ahead: I'll make a mental note if she reacts better or worse to this approach.

The Challenge of Empathizing

Sometimes empathizing with your teen is easier said than done. We encourage you to review the questions under our description of Empathy (page 49) to help generate other possibilities as to why your teen may be acting in a certain way. However, we also recognize that it is difficult to come up with a lot of other possibilities, so we encourage you to talk to others who may be somewhat removed from your situation and could lend an objective ear and mind to understanding and responding in new ways to your teen's behavior. It may be helpful, for example, to talk to other parents of teens (whether or not the teens are depressed).

Empathizing with and understanding teens can require a very different set of skills from empathizing with younger children. Talk to someone who has recently made this transition. We are often surprised in our parenting groups at the situations raised that "stump" the therapists but are easily understood by other parents.

If understanding your teen's motives is difficult, it may also help to review reasons that are *unlikely* to motivate his behavior. The following are some common myths about teen motivation:

- *He's doing it because he hates me."* Teens may become angry or even enraged with their parents, but (except in cases of extreme child abuse) they almost never consistently hate them. Usually, the anger is temporary and results from frustration with a particular situation. Sometimes, negative behavior can also result from a misguided bid for parental attention, whether or not the teen is aware of this motivation. For example, after his father started a new job that involved considerable business travel, a fifteen-year-old boy left a small bag of marijuana in plain view on the desk in his bedroom. He later admitted he was glad his father found it, and talked about wanting to spend more time with him.

- *"He can't help it. It's just his character."* Young teens do not have fully developed, stable personalities. Even older teens still need to undergo considerable change and emotional development. Think about it: how many people in your own high school class are still pursuing the careers they said they would pursue at graduation? To be helpful to your teen, it works better to focus on his strengths and potential for change, rather than seeing him as permanently flawed in some way.

- *"He's just listening to his peers and there's nothing I can do about it."* While it is true that peers become more influential at adolescence, parents' views still matter to teens. In fact, many teens have told us they want their parents more involved, not less involved, in providing guidance and support in their lives. For these teens, joining an antisocial peer group may be a cry for help rather than a rejection of their parents.

- *"She knows exactly what she's doing. She's pushing my buttons on purpose."* Teens sometimes don't know why they do certain things. They may be responding to their parents in negative ways that have become a habit, and have no idea why this keeps happening. They may not have thought about alternative ways of dealing with their parents, or may find the alternatives too difficult. Deliberate attempts to harass parents are rare. When they occur, they usually stem from resentment over a recent unresolved parent-teen conflict. For example, Suzy was upset that her mother didn't buy her the dress she really wanted, so she "accidentally" spilled grape juice on the one her mother had chosen.

Attitudes and Actions That Have Already Been Helpful

Think about two or three difficult behaviors in your teen that you think *may* be related to depression. What responses have you already found helpful? Remember, it doesn't have to be a total solution to the problem, just something that had even a small positive effect on your child's (or your own) behavior. Write down as many helpful responses as you can on the last page of the chapter (or photocopy the page first, if you don't own the book). Then, insert your favorite one in the "L.E.A.P." plan space to remind you to do it this week.

Examples of helpful responses from other parents:
- Extra patience;
- Perseverance;
- Leaving the situation for a period of time;
- Not losing one's temper;
- Removing distractions (for example, when doing homework);
- Allowing for the natural consequences of his/her choice (as long as they are not dangerous);
- Using diversions or rewards;

My spouse and I both work. Where do we find the time to do this?

Most L.E.A.P. plans are not "add-ons" to your life. Instead, they represent different ways of relating to your teen. Since you relate to your depressed teen every day anyway, you might as well do it in a way that leaves you feeling positive and might actually help! The only additional time you need for this approach is about fifteen minutes per week to evaluate how it's going and decide whether or not you want to modify your plan the next week. We usually suggest doing this with your spouse or a significant other, if possible (the old idea that "two heads are better than one"), but it can be done on your own or certainly with the help of a trusted friend or family member, if you are a single parent.

- Using one's own experience to help kids overcome problems. (This suggestion was accompanied by a cautionary note on how to do it wisely: Don't offer "when I was a boy…" tall tales, but share similar experiences in order to show empathy or to suggest options for the youngster on how to deal with a situation).

Now It's Your Turn!

For the topic presented in each chapter, you'll be encouraged to think about specific situations that might be addressed using a L.E.A.P. plan. At the end of each chapter, there is space to add your L.E.A.P. plan response. Writing it down will reduce the chances of forgetting it. The response doesn't have to be fancy: any new idea that you plan to try out that week is fine. Don't forget the first two steps, though. Make sure you've thought about your own feelings about the situation you're addressing, and that you've also thought about it from your child's point of view (empathy). Each subsequent chapter will include a reminder to do "P": follow-up on the previous week's results and do further planning.

Also note that some parents find it helpful to work on the same L.E.A.P plan for several consecutive weeks before moving on to another one. That's fine too. In fact, it may be advisable to do this at least once, if dealing with a particularly difficult area. Your goal is not to create fifteen L.E.A.P. plans, but to follow up on at least one constructive idea for change in relation to your teen.

Key Points

The situation: _____

_____

_____

Write down responses that have already helped: _____

_____

_____

Your L.E.A.P. plan response for this week is:

Label your thoughts and feelings: _____

_____

_____

_____

Empathize with your teen: _____

_____

_____

_____

Explore ways to respond: _____

_____

_____

_____

Apply alternative idea/plan: _____

_____

_____

_____

Pick a follow-up time: _____

_____

_____

_____

Plan ahead: _____

_____

_____

_____

Part

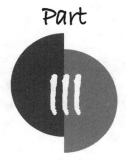

III

The
L.E.A.P. Approach
and Your Teen

Lights, Camera, Action!

In the previous chapter, we introduced the concept of L.E.A.P. plans and asked you to try developing one. We didn't give you any particular guidance as to what to focus your L.E.A.P. plan on. Perhaps you chose the behavior that was most troubling to you, or one that seemed as if it was fairly minor and perhaps easy to resolve. Starting in this chapter, we are going to begin highlighting areas that are often difficult for teens with depression and suggest ways that L.E.A.P. plans can help you improve your teen's functioning in this area. For example, in this chapter, the focus is on increasing activity in your depressed teen: a challenge for many parents.

> **Progress Check**
>
> Any progress with the L.E.A.P. plan you started last week? Remember, it's OK to repeat one for several weeks if you're working on an important change. In fact, to keep things simple, it's probably best not to do more than two plans at any given time.

Timothy (continued): *"Why do they just sit there feeling sorry for themselves?" asked the mother of Timothy, the boy with dysthymic disorder described earlier. Apparently, Timothy's repeated exclamations of "I'm no good at anything!" were beginning to try her patience.*

Consistent with Timothy's behavior, one reason for depressed teens to "sit around feeling sorry for themselves" is *learned helplessness:* the belief that one cannot succeed at anything, so there is no point in trying. There are other reasons too, though. Mood problems often lead to low energy and low desire for social interaction, resulting in sitting around at home. Another possibility is that the moody teen is thinking about problems over and over again (called "rumination"). This mental habit is common in people with mood problems because it creates the illusion of doing something about their problems, and raises hopes of solving them. Unfortunately, the opposite is often true. Rumination usually results in worse depression and fails to solve problems. Therefore, it is important to try to interrupt this mental habit whenever possible and reinforce constructive activity.

The Importance of Activity

Today we begin to look at the importance of activity in overcoming depressed mood. This can include physical activities, activities that involve other people, or simply a pastime that is harmless and enjoyable to your teen. We advise trying to increase your teen's activity first before we advise having your teen look at his own depressive thinking. This is because studies have shown that the introspection associated with looking at depressive thinking can actually make mood *worse* if introduced too soon.

The beneficial effect of activity on mood is often underestimated, yet we know:

- Aerobic exercise (i.e., exercise that is vigorous enough to consistently increase your heart rate) prevents depression and depressive relapse.
- Activity that involves others reduces withdrawal and increases emotional support.
- Enjoyable activities help overcome depressive *anhedonia* (the inability to enjoy things).
- Any activity interferes with depressive rumination (the tendency to think too much about oneself and one's life).
- Activity interferes with maladaptive coping and unhealthy distractions (such as drugs or Internet sleaze).

How Do We Get Them Moving?

Helping depressed teens increase their activity level can be a major challenge. In general, start with what they're most willing or least resistant to doing. It doesn't have to be a major athletic event. Anything that gets them moving is OK. Getting up and brushing your teeth is better than staying in bed all day or lying in front of the television! In fact, insisting on a few basic routines is often the place to start. Beyond that, parents have told us that they've had better luck with activities that involve a particular interest the child cares about, or a good friend or group of friends. Solitary, inactive pursuits like Gameboy are less ideal, but can still be used (in moderation) to reward doing more challenging activities.

Expect "two steps forward/one step back," as there will be good days and bad days initially. Ignore setbacks and cheer the positives. Remind your teen that he did the activity before, to instill confidence that he can do it again. Also, expect mornings to be worst (that's just part of depression). Get an alarm clock and make sure it's on the opposite side of the room from the bed, so he can't shut it off until he gets out of bed.

Be realistic and encourage every tiny step in the right direction. For example, even resuming basic self-care activities that have been abandoned recently is progress.

Help your teen prioritize to avoid unnecessary stress. For example, one or two after school activities may have to go temporarily, in order to maintain the more "basic" activities such as getting to school. You want your child to become more active, but he can't resume everything from one day to the next. If you build up the activity level gradually, he is much more likely to persevere without becoming overwhelmed or discouraged.

Try to maintain the attitude "I'm encouraging activity because it's good for my teen, even though it's not easy for him or her to do," rather than "He has to get moving because I need to get back to work" or "He has to stop moping around because it's driving me nuts." The latter statements may be true, but they will make you more frustrated and more likely to get into nonproductive arguments about activity. The first attitude will keep you focused on empathic approaches, which are less likely to meet with resistance from your teen.

What If My Child Fights Me When I Try to Get Him Out of His Room?

Gradual involvement in the outside world may be needed, to keep your child from feeling overwhelmed. Be positive about every footstep out the door and build up time "outside" in gradual steps. You may have to fight or drag the teen when it comes to essentials (for example, doctor's appointments to decide about medication adjustments), but try to avoid doing this daily. A positive incentive for time spent outside the room often works better, with a bonus for actually doing something there (for example, going to the store, making a phone call, or doing anything more than sitting on the couch). Try to offer something your teen likes whenever he does something, rather than negotiating about it beforehand. Some teens will feel coerced if you try to get them involved in a reward "system," but won't mind an extra "surprise" dollar when offered (or extra Nintendo time, extra privilege, visit from a friend—whatever is motivating). Sincere praise and acknowledgment of progress are great incentives too.

If your child appears "stuck" in his room for days despite your best efforts, you may require outside help. First, see if he is willing to go out in the company of a friend or family member. Going for a walk with someone familiar is a nice, natural way to resume outdoor activity. If this fails, seek professional help. If you fear your child may harm himself in his room, you may be able to call emergency services and get him seen at the local hospital. If this is not the case, it is unlikely that a doctor or psychologist will come to your home, as they are rarely paid to do so. Arranging some visits by a Child and Youth Worker or Child Youth Associate can be an excellent alternative in this case. These professionals usually have received training in managing difficult behavior and many have experience dealing with depressed teens. Check out their specific experience and credentials. You may have to hire them yourself, but the expense is well worth it if they help you overcome this hurdle with your teen.

Suggestions from Other Parents

- Model an active lifestyle. For example, even if you're not a sports enthusiast, you can walk to the corner store instead of taking the car, or walk up a flight or two of stairs instead of waiting for the elevator.
- Establish routines for sleeping, eating, exercise, school, and homework. Routines typically improve one's energy level throughout the day, making it easier to engage in other activities.
- Encourage the most minimal activity (for example, say, "That's more than you did yesterday; keep it up").
- Do the activity with your teen.
- Involve a friend or sibling.
- Remember what your child used to enjoy and make it easy to get back into it.
- Ask about a "daily highlight" at the end of the day. This is something that was either enjoyable for your teen or represented a step forward (and can be anything he does or experiences that's legal).
- "When you do it, then we'll have a treat" (Grandma's rule).
- Set a limit on "down time" in his room (for example, set the computer up outside the bedroom, so the only reason for him to go into his room is to sleep).
- Allow the natural consequences of inaction (for example, if your teen doesn't go to the fridge, he doesn't eat).
- Be a persistent "cheerleader" for activity (don't yell or argue).
- Buy or rent an enticing new game, ball, etc. that your teen might like to try.
- Organize family trips to places he might grudgingly go along to such as the beach, the park, or a ball game.

Using L.E.A.P. Plans to Encourage Activity

Let's go back to Timothy now (the boy at the beginning of the chapter who kept saying "I'm not good at anything"), and see how his mother applied a L.E.A.P. plan. Timothy's mother was concerned that he did a lot of sitting and very little physical activity. His mother found his "moping around feeling sorry for himself" annoying and frustrating. She developed a L.E.A.P. plan to help Timothy get more exercise (and for her to get more peace of mind!).

L:

Label your thoughts and feelings: I am *so frustrated* with his lack of interest in sports or activities. I wish he would embrace an activity that would get his blood flowing! I am so *worried* about his lack of exercise and moping around. Feeling sorry for himself like that will just make his depression worse!

E:

Empathize with your teen: Timothy has always gotten frustrated easily and said "I'm no good at that!" Maybe his saying "I'm no good at anything!" is just an extreme version of this. He may not be feeling sorry for himself, just feeling unusually frustrated. Exercise has always been a challenge for him. He has no sports-related interests, so it may not be realistic to expect him to embrace activity.

Explore ways to respond: If Timothy's frustrated, it doesn't make sense to get frustrated back at him. Instead, maybe I could just say, matter-of-factly, "You sound frustrated," and then suggest something we could do together to take his mind off it. He loves animals and I usually am the one to walk the dog. Maybe we could start with a small step like walking the dog together. I could even chip in a little cash to motivate him. Maybe in time if he gets more active and feels better, I can encourage him to take it on more like an odd job, walking other people's dogs. He also loves nature and fishing. Fishing is just sitting, though. But if I encourage fishing with his Dad combined with a nature walk, he'll get some exercise!

A:

Apply alternate idea/plan: I am going to first suggest fishing with his Dad, and take him along on the occasional dog walk. Then, a week or so later, I am going to ask him if he would like to take on a new job to walk Lassie.

P:

Pick a follow up time and plan ahead: Each week on Saturday I am going to note changes, even small ones. I am also going to run my ideas by my husband.

This is an excellent example of how Timothy's mother used her knowledge of his personality and interests to develop new activities for him that involved some exercise. She was also careful not to rush in with her solutions and she made a plan to evaluate and follow-up.

Sometimes, it's important to take into account the teen's own wishes when encouraging activity. The example below illustrates this point.

Jerry and His Yearbook Interest: *Jerry really thrived on being able to contribute to the yearbook, but couldn't concentrate on his math. His parents wanted to forbid yearbook activities until math was done, but this was demoralizing because the math never got done and one of the few things Jerry enjoyed was yearbook. We* *decided the benefits of being able to contribute to something outweighed the risk of failing math. Jerry's yearbook work contributed to his self-esteem and facilitated recovery from depression, and he got his math credit at summer school once his mood had improved.*

Exercise: Increasing Activity

Depressed teens are often not motivated to engage in activities. This chapter reviewed some ways to help motivate them. List your favorite two at the end of the chapter and do a L.E.A.P. plan that includes at least one.

Because it can be hard to remember to encourage activity on a regular basis, you may also wish to use the table provided at the end of this chapter, at least initially, to record when you do so. You can then reinforce both yourself and your teen if there is even the slightest movement. Try not to nag repeatedly, as this may increase your teen's resistance to movement. Encourage once, using one of the strategies mentioned above, and be positive about every action you see, literally. Make further copies of the table if you would like to keep encouraging in subsequent weeks. Seeing activity level gradually build up can be very encouraging to both you and your teen.

Key Points

- Activity helps depressed teens, but they can be difficult to motivate.

- Take the attitude "I'm encouraging activity because it's good for my teen, even though it's hard for him or her to do."

- Remember to positively reinforce every tiny step he takes.

- Don't forget to reinforce the "realistic positives" your teen is already doing, listed back in Chapter 2!

- List two ideas for increasing activity you'd like to try with your teen:

1. _____

2. _____

Your L.E.A.P. plan response for this week is:

The situation: _____

_____

_____

_____

_____

Label your thoughts and feelings: _____

_____

_____

_____

_____

Empathize with your teen: _____

_____

_____

_____

_____

Explore ways to respond: _____

_____

_____

_____

_____

Apply alternative idea/plan: _____

_____

_____

_____

_____

Pick a follow-up time and plan ahead: _____

_____

_____

_____

_____

Action Encouraged	Date Done	Result	Did I Remember to Reinforce It (yes/no)

Healthy Habits

Today we will talk about something very basic to recovering from depression: good health habits. The mind and the body are very closely linked, so in order to feel better emotionally, most people must feel physically better as well. To improve physical well-being, the healthy eating, sleeping, hygiene, and relaxation habits described in this chapter can really help. Although it's not directly linked to health, the habit of school attendance is also essential for children and teens, so we devote an additional section to this habit. As mentioned before, it takes a good six weeks (for anyone, let alone someone who is depressed) to make a new habit, so be patient when your teen is working on these habits. Last week, we started to work on the "activity habit." Let's look at some more specific habits.

> **A Chubby Group:** *In one group for depressed teens, we noticed that there was one extremely thin boy (depression had suppressed his appetite), but the other participants were uniformly overweight. Even prior to depression, their exercise and eating habits had been poor. Moreover, on meeting the parent group, it was obvious that they too could benefit from some healthy changes in these areas. To foster better eating habits in the teens, we encouraged their parents to bring healthy snacks to the group each week.*

These observations are not meant to be insulting to our treatment group; merely to illustrate that modeling has a powerful effect in modulating day-to-day habits. You

Progress Check

Let's review the action table from last week, and see what can be learned from it. Most parents notice variability from day to day in their teens' activity level. This is to be expected, as depressed moods often fluctuate day to day as well. Teens who are attending school may feel exhausted by the weekend, given the energy-depleting effect of depression. Other teens may show the opposite pattern, as they feel more optimistic when temporarily relieved of school stress. Whatever the pattern, you are trying to record effort here: your effort to encourage, and your teen's to respond. As much as possible, ignore the negative and focus on the positive. If you got even minimal responses last week, carry on!

Note that you will be doing two L.E.A.P. plans at the same time by the end of this chapter. If you didn't get any response last week, talk to your spouse or another adult who knows your teen well about how to encourage her more effectively. If possible, ask the professional working with your teen the same question. Sometimes it simply takes a few weeks for other interventions to begin working, and then teens respond more readily to parental encouragement.

may already know a great deal about maintaining a healthy body weight, and perhaps you do not have a weight problem personally. Nevertheless, we know that large numbers of children and teens in North America are becoming obese, and that eating habits established at an early age tend to persist into adulthood. Therefore, encouraging and modeling healthy eating for our children is relevant to their future, whether they are depressed or not.

Parents who adopt healthy lifestyles are more likely to have children and teens who adopt healthy lifestyles. Parents can also create the means to change unhealthy habits. For example, they can promote healthy eating by often shopping for fresh fruit rather than stocking the cupboards with pop and chips. They can ensure that bicycles and other sports equipment are in good repair. Teens don't always have the financial resources to make these changes. Here are some further thoughts on food habits.

Food Habits

Depression can result in increased or decreased appetite. In addition, some depressed teens have cravings for sweets or other "junk." Eating disorders are also a prevalent problem in teens, and can sometimes coexist with depression. Major changes in weight need to be discussed with a doctor, but try not to monitor every morsel that passes your teen's lips. For many teens, food is an area where they like to assert some personal choice, and becoming overly focused on their choices can increase (not decrease) the risk of eating disorders. Some general suggestions for fostering healthier eating include:

- *Avoid power struggles around food:* healthy food choices should be encouraged (for example, by pointing out money saved when snacking on fruit at home instead of going to the store for junk food), and unhealthy ones ignored.

- *Keep healthy snacks in the house and within easy reach;* limit junk food in the house.
- *Accept that you have little control of what teens eat outside the house,* but point out the financial benefits of not spending one's allowance on snacks. Allowance at this age should also be earned, at least in part, to further discourage frivolous spending.
- Eating in front of the television tends to exacerbate food problems (i.e., overeaters eat more; undereaters eat less). Parents should set the example with this and *have rules about where and when food can be eaten in the house.*

If your depressed teen is eating less:
- *Monitor fluid intake.* Drinking too little results in medical emergencies more often than eating too little. If your teen doesn't like large glasses of juice or water, offer her some bottled water to sip on during the day. Alternatively, offer her foods that contain lots of fluid like Jello, popsicles, or watermelon.
- *Regular check-ups with a medical doctor* are indicated if your teen's weight or health is unstable. Ask the doctor how regularly your teen should be monitored.
- For low appetite, *allow some flexibility on when to eat and how much is consumed at each time,* as long as the total intake over twenty-four hours is enough.
- *Meal routines can help those who "forget" to eat.* Depressed teens with low appetite often claim to forget meals. Rather than challenging this claim, gently but consistently remind your teen of mealtimes.
- *Aim for the four basic food groups each day* (fruits and vegetables; breads and cereals; meat, fish, or other protein; dairy products), rather than counting calories. Modest goals are needed, especially in more acutely depressed teens. There is also some recent evidence suggesting that a diet high in fish and low in cholesterol may contribute to improved mood in depression. If you can cook this way and your teen eats at home at least some of the time, this diet may be helpful.

Sleep Habits

Most healthy teens sleep an average of about eight hours a night (give or take an hour), as adults do. Younger teens may sleep a bit more. Regardless of the time spent asleep, though, healthy teens awaken with enough energy to face the day. Even if morning is not their favorite time, they are able to get through the day without fatigue, and they participate in school and other activities without falling asleep. Sleep is important to allow participation in those activities, to ensure good concentration, and to give the body a chance to repair itself.

Sleep is often disturbed in depression. Falling asleep can be difficult, especially if your child is anxious, and early wakening is typical in major depression. Some depressed teens sleep excessively too, contributing to lethargy and inactivity. Many teens (whether depressed or not) struggle with sleep cycle problems. Typically, they stay up too late (studying, watching TV, socializing) and then can't get out of bed in the morning. They try to "catch up" with an after-school nap, resulting in another late night and establishing a pattern of late sleeping. Some good rules for improving sleep include:

- *Don't take naps during the day.*
- *Find a reasonable bedtime and stick to it,* give or take fifteen minutes. Bear in mind that going to sleep too early can isolate you further from friends; too late can interfere with school performance the next day.
- *Establish a regular bedtime routine* (it helps "cue" the body for sleep). For example, when taking a shower, changing into pajamas, and doing some light reading all predictably precede sleep every night, the body begins preparing for sleep at the start of that routine, and sleep comes more quickly.
- *Keep to a regular wake time, even on weekends* (or at least within half an hour on weekends, as this keeps the habit going). Many teens can see the logic of this approach, as it will reduce the "Monday morning blahs" they otherwise experience, but it's not worth a fight if they do not.
- *Don't consume any caffeine after lunch.*
- *Stay away from alcohol and illegal drugs.*
- *Don't participate in stimulating activities after dinner* (for example, avoid Nintendo or fighting with the family). Exercise should conclude a couple of hours before bedtime as well, but this may not always be possible if a child participates in sports teams that have late games or practices.
- *Do some daily relaxation activities* (see below).
- *Take part in regular physical exercise,* especially aerobic activity that gets the heart pumping faster, but not during the last couple of hours before bedtime.
- *Try taking a warm bath or eating cereal and milk* (which contain natural sleep-inducers), or other benign remedies before bedtime.
- Remember: It's not the end of the world to miss a night of sleep. Worrying about sleeplessness only makes it worse.

Antidepressant medications can either increase or decrease sleep. Usually, the more activating medications are given in the morning, and the more sedating ones in the evening to minimize sleep disturbance. Sleep disturbances during the first week or two on medication are common, and often subside. However, if your child's sleep is consistently worse (i.e., for more than two weeks) after starting medication, talk to the doctor. Either the timing, the dose, or the type of medication may have to be changed to allow your child to benefit while maintaining adequate sleep.

Going to School

The longer teens are out of school, the harder it is for them to return. Ideally, treatment for depression should occur while your child attends school, and you can discuss with her teachers the possibility of modified academic expectations for the duration of her illness. In severe depression, regular school attendance may not be possible. If your teen has been absent for a while, make a plan with the school and other professionals involved to ease the transition back. Some suggestions that may be included in the plan are:

- *Have a morning routine,* so that all essential activities are done at approximately the same time before school.
- Prepare or have your teen *prepare necessary items the night before* (lunch, book-bag, etc.)
- Some families *use a kitchen timer to help their teen stay on schedule* with dressing, eating, and other morning activities, using an enjoyable but brief activity to provide a natural reward for beating the timer (often, ten or fifteen minutes of a favorite television show; alternatively, a video game of similar duration).
- *Let your teen return to school in small steps if she hasn't gone in a while.* A brief visit may be the place to start, followed by attending one or two classes, and then gradually more. Reintegration may take a few weeks, and (ideally) the teen should have some say over the pace of change.
- *Your teen may need to have an adult accompany her to school, at least initially, to ensure she arrives there.* A friend can take over this role eventually, to reduce any embarrassment about being chaperoned.
- *See work completion as a secondary goal, and the ability to return to class as primary.* Academic success is "icing on the cake" when trying to return a teen to school after a serious bout with depression.
- *Plan how to deal with embarrassing questions from peers or teachers about school absence or about the illness.* Rehearse with your teen one or two socially acceptable responses to these questions that are not too far from the truth, but limit embarrassment. "I was sick, but now I'm getting better" or "I felt too crummy to go to school" are simple responses, but ask what your teen prefers as well. If a very stressful event occurred preceding the depression, your teen might refer back to this event. For example, "I was depressed about my father/friend dying."
- *Reinforce every little step in the right direction, at least at home.* Teacher praise for attendance is often too embarrassing, but

teachers can monitor progress and, once informed, parents can
offer praise at home.

Also see Chapter 16 on working with schools.

Relaxation

Although relaxation techniques were originally developed for those with anxiety
disorders, teens with depression can also benefit from them. The most basic technique is called "diaphragmatic breathing," to indicate that the muscle at the base
of the lungs (diaphragm) is involved. Because this muscle is connected to nerves
that are part of the body's autonomic (involuntary) nervous system, stretching
this muscle triggers a natural relaxation response. To do this technique, start by
breathing *slowly:* allow the air to go in through the nose and out through the
mouth, either while lying or sitting straight with shoulders down. Put a hand on
your belly. If the air is going to the diaphragm, your hand should move out a little
on the in-breath, and fall back on the out-breath. Count to four on every in-breath
if it's hard to slow down. If you feel dizzy or get a pins-and-needles sensation,
you're breathing too fast. When you've practiced this technique yourself, see if
your teen is willing to do it with you.

Here are some tips to encourage relaxation:

- Eli Bay (see Bibliography) has excellent relaxation tapes to listen
  to, if your teen is willing to try these.
- Activities that include relaxed breathing (martial arts, yoga,
  singing) are great too.
- Doing relaxation techniques with your child or teen makes it less
  of a chore, and may be helpful to you, too!
- A few minutes a day of regular practice is needed for two to three
  weeks to master the technique. Bedtime is usually the best time to
  practice, as it can improve quality and quantity of sleep in some
  teens as well.
- Once this type of breathing comes naturally to you and your teen,
  encourage breathing this way during the day whenever she is
  starting to feel tense. It doesn't work when very "worked up," but
  is good for anticipatory anxiety (i.e., worrying about something
  ahead of time) or mild irritability.

Hygiene Habits

Maia and Body Odor: *Maia is fourteen and quite physically mature for her age.
She and her mother had a talk some time ago about the importance of deodorant.
Initially, Maia was quite thrilled about the idea of using deodorant and the implicit
meaning it had in "growing up." However, over the past year, Maia has experienced*

some significant losses and now experiences dysthymia. Over the year, she has taken less and less care of herself. The deodorant has gone by the wayside. Often when Maia comes home from school, her mom is mortified at the smell of Maia's body odor.

Before meeting with parents of depressed teens, we had no idea we would be writing about deodorant. Nevertheless, several parents we spoke to reported that poor hygiene (bowel or bladder "accidents," not using deodorant, not changing clothes for several days at a time, failure to bathe, shower, or brush their teeth, etc.) was a major concern. This makes sense, as depression reduces one's sense of self-worth, and people who feel poorly about themselves are less likely to take care of themselves. Some suggestions include:

- See the family doctor if you're not sure whether there is a physical cause for the hygiene problem (for example, severe constipation, "accidents," or other unusual bowel/bladder habits).
- Provide regular reminders to do these habits (depressed kids sometimes don't think about self-care) or provide a written checklist.
- Do some self-care with your teen (for example, brushing hair or brushing teeth together) until she begins to do it regularly again on her own.
- Say: "You deserve to look pretty"; "You deserve to smell nice"; "You look/smell great!"
- Provide praise for the results of better hygiene. For example, "You look great today!"
- Make the bathroom fun (improving the decor, getting a new bath oil, etc.).
- Model the joys of good hygiene. For example, point out how relaxing you find a hot shower or bath, or try some "aromatherapy" with fragrant shower gels and comment on how it wakes you up in the morning.
- If all else fails or if your teen says, "I don't care about any of this," allow the natural consequences. (Usually, peer rejection occurs, which may increase her motivation to improve hygiene).

Now, let's see how Maia's mother applied a L.E.A.P. plan to the deodorant problem.

Label your own thoughts and feelings: I can't understand how Maia can be at school and not care about smelling! I am so *embarrassed!* What do people think of her? What do they think of me? I *feel sorry* for her. The other girls (not to mention boys) must notice and be appalled! And the teacher!

Empathize with your teen: If I were in her shoes and felt her low mood, I might feel like not bothering either. Maybe she doesn't feel worth smelling nice and looking pretty.

Explore ways to respond: Maybe I need to help her get back into the habit of using deodorant by talking with her in an empathetic way.

Apply alternative idea/plan: I am going to start by saying something like this, "Maia, you are a lovely kid. I am proud of the person that you are. You are pretty and look great with your blue jeans and your new white blouse. There is one thing that I want to mention to you. Last year, when you were not experiencing these low moods, you used deodorant regularly and always smelled fresh and clean. In the past few months, you've let that go…maybe because you don't care as much, or maybe you don't feel as pretty. I am not sure, but I do understand it has been really tough these past few months. I want you to feel better about yourself. Would it be OK if I give you gentle reminders to use your deodorant? I don't want this to become a bad habit for you. And, sometimes you don't notice yourself that you have body odor but others do! So, I don't want you losing friends over a bad habit!"

I will try to get her agreement to use a private signal to supportively remind her to use deodorant. Maybe I will buy a few different kinds so she can try some new scents. I will praise her (but not embarrass her) by my words and gestures when she looks and smells clean!

Pick a follow up time and plan ahead: I will check in with her once next week on Friday to see how our plan is working.

Notice how this mother focuses on the positives before offering her suggestion. She also demonstrates empathy in her approach ("I am not sure, but I do understand it has been really tough these past few months"). She also engages Maia in coming up with a solution together. Collaborating with your teen can go a long way.

Exercise: Improving a Habit

What good health habits do you already practice? Which ones does your child also practice? Which ones are problem areas for your child? Is this because of depression, or has it always been a problem? It's easier to get back into a good habit that your child used to have than to establish a new one, so start working with the one(s) that your child used to do. How can you encourage a habit empathically? It may help to acknowledge that we all struggle with establishing good habits from time to time, so you might as well admit it's not easy. After this admission, mention how you keep yourself on track. See if you can develop a L.E.A.P. plan for fostering a good health habit.

Key Points

Write down a couple of ideas to try for the one habit that you think your child could improve with your help. If you're stuck, review the bulleted suggestion list for that habit in the chapter.

_____

_____

_____

_____

_____

_____

_____

_____

Your L.E.A.P. plan response for this week is:

The situation: _____
_____
_____
_____
_____

Label your thoughts and feelings: _____
_____
_____
_____
_____

Empathize with your teen: _____
_____
_____
_____
_____

Explore ways to respond: _____
_____
_____
_____
_____

Apply alternative idea/plan: _____
_____
_____
_____
_____

Pick a follow-up time and plan ahead: _____
_____
_____
_____
_____

Depressive Thinking

Most people think of depression as a feeling, but thoughts connected with that feeling can be equally troubling. When people are depressed, their thoughts go from "bad to worse." They take every minor problem or setback they encounter and see it as a sign that things can never go right for them again. A depressed teen might get a bad grade on a test, for example, and conclude that he will fail his year.

Fortunately, changing thinking patterns for the better can also change mood for the better, as we will see in this chapter. Patience is needed, though, because teens often need to work on basic life skills like those discussed in the last couple of chapters (maintaining routines, good health habits, going to school, becoming more active) before they can benefit from changing their thinking. Trying to work on thinking too soon can undermine progress by getting depressed teens overly focused on their thoughts (the unhealthy habit of rumination, discussed in an earlier chapter). If your teen is making good progress in the basic skills already discussed, however, it may be worthwhile to start paying attention to his thinking.

Janice (continued): *Janice, described in the Introduction, often told her mother about her thoughts and feelings when she called her at work. Initially, her mother was happy that her daughter was so open and honest about her feelings. It was a welcome change from the stories of "silent, sullen teens" she heard from her*

Progress Check

You may be working on several L.E.A.P. plans at this point—perhaps one to increase activity and one to improve health habits. It's usually best not to do more than about two plans at any given time, because you or your teen may lose track of them, feel overburdened, or not complete them. Once there is good progress with a L.E.A.P. plan, it should require less thought and start to feel more natural. Once you reach this point, the plan is becoming more of a habit for you and your teen, and you are probably ready to focus on a new one.

Did you follow up on a L.E.A.P. plan this week? When? Will you continue the same one this week? Continue it with modification? Try something new? If uncertain, involve your spouse or partner in the discussion. Two heads are better than one!

co-workers. Eventually, though, she got frustrated with Janice's attitude, because nothing she said seemed to help change it. Every day it was the same story: "Oh Mom, I can't do anything right. I missed the last two classes yesterday, and Mr. Jones gave a surprise quiz. There's another 20 percent of my grade down the drain. I'll probably fail now. What a loser I am. Even the other kids are starting to notice. Alicia never calls any more, and Lauren has started hanging around with that weirdo Jane. I'm sure they've written me off. Might as well go to bed and never get up again. I don't know what to do anymore...."

If her mother then suggested some things to do, Janice found reasons why her suggestions couldn't possibly work, and therefore were not even worth trying. Eventually, the conversation concluded with, "I have to get back to work, dear, but do the best you can. We'll talk again tonight". Needless to say, the evening conversation was no different than the phone call at work.

How Thinking Affects Mood

Depressed teens often engage in negative thinking, which means taking a negative or ambiguous event, seeing it as worse than it really was, and then focusing on various catastrophic consequences it might have. This process is sometimes described as a "negative thinking spiral."

Negative thinking spirals can make mood worse. They are usually characterized by exaggerating the negative, ignoring the positive, going from bad to worse (taking a problem situation and thinking only about the worst possible outcome), and thinking in absolutes (for example, "If things aren't great, they are terrible"). For instance, a depressed teen who is teased will often think, "Everybody hates me" (exaggerating the negative), rather than, "Sam doesn't like me." In response to getting 8 out of 10 right on a quiz, the same teen might think "Oh no! Where did I lose the two points?" (ignoring the positive) rather than "I got a B!"

These thinking patterns are involuntary, and change once depression is adequately treated. Telling someone to "snap out of it" doesn't work, because this is a brain characteristic associated with depression. Brain imaging techniques have actually shown changes in brain functioning with depression that resolve with successful treatment.

The result of this negative thinking is a distorted perception of oneself as worthless, others as uncaring, and the future as hopeless. Many years ago, Aaron Beck, a psychologist, described the triangle of worthless self, uncaring world, and hopeless future, and developed a treatment for depression based on altering negative thinking. This triangle provides a nice way to summarize the depressed state of mind. Think about it as you try to understand your depressed teen.

To illustrate the effect of the depressed state of mind, try the following. Think about something that happened to you in the past week that didn't turn out as well as you had hoped it would. For example, you didn't get the raise you applied for at work. Rate how you felt at the time (from 1-10, where 1 is terrible and 10 is wonderful).

Now assume:
- It was completely your fault.
- It reflects some permanent flaw in either your character or your intelligence (whichever you value more).
- This flaw supersedes all your other characteristics and will therefore ruin your life.
- You are therefore doomed to eternal failure and rejection.

Now rate how you feel (1-10).

Now assume:
- The problem was at least partly due to circumstances or someone else's mistake.
- The problem represents a temporary setback for an otherwise successful, likeable person.
- Even if the problem can't be fixed, there are other situations that are bound to turn out better.
- Therefore, in the grand scheme of things, it's really not that big a deal.

Now rate how you feel (1-10).

If the last number is even a little higher than the previous one, you have just demonstrated the powerful effect thoughts can have on feelings. This effect is described in an approach to depression termed "cognitive therapy" or "cognitive-behavioral therapy" (CBT). This book is written from a cognitive-behavioral perspective because, although the therapeutic techniques take considerable training, the basic principles are fairly simple and can be applied readily to parenting teens.

The way CBT works is by identifying the distortions in one's thinking, or just identifying "down thinking" in general, and then doing something about it. (This could include either stopping the spiral and distracting oneself, engaging in a constructive or enjoyable activity, or correcting the distortion and replacing it with more realistic thoughts.) Note that CBT is meant to get the teen thinking realistically, not necessarily "rosy." Some teens do have problems that need to be dealt with, and just thinking optimistically will not change them. For example, if a depressed boy thinks Mr. Jackson is angry with him because he skipped Mr. Jackson's class three out of five days last week, that is reality. It is *not* a cognitive distortion in need of CBT. In this case, the solution is for the boy to go to Mr. Jackson, face the music, and agree to improve his attendance.

How Can Parents Encourage More Realistic Thinking?

Imagine that you were Janice's mother. What would you do? Here is a L.E.A.P. plan Janice's mother used to deal with her depressive thinking:

Label feelings/thoughts: I feel *frustrated* that Janice keeps complaining and doesn't act on any of my suggestions. I also feel *responsible* when she says, "I'm a loser," because I don't like to see myself as a parent who has raised "a loser." This feeling makes me want to convince her that she's not a loser, and then we end up arguing.

Empathize with your teen: I haven't really raised a loser. That's just Janice's depression talking. The lack of action in response to my suggestions may also relate to depression. After all, when she was not depressed and had more energy, Janice usually followed through on her commitments.

Explore ways to respond: Maybe, instead of arguing, I could say, "It sounds like you're getting discouraged, but you've handled situations like this before," or, "You only feel like a loser because of the depression. Even though you're depressed, there might still be something you could do." Then, I could put the ball back in her court and ask, "What's worked for you before in this situation?" or, "How can I help?" If she can't come up with an idea, maybe I could offer several and ask her to choose one that sounds OK to her. In her present state of mind, I'm not expecting enthusiasm, just a grunt of acknowledgment. Even if Janice only says a word or two, I can congratulate her for taking part in finding a solution.

Apply alternative idea/plan: I'll combine a couple of these ideas. "It sounds like you're getting discouraged, but you've handled situations like this before" avoids the word "depression" (which she hates) and gives her a nice vote of confidence. "What's worked for you before in this situation?" followed by some choices may help too. I can certainly be positive about any step she's willing to take. Talking this way should also interrupt her depressive thinking for a while.

Pick a follow up time and plan ahead: I'll try doing this consistently when Janice calls this week, and review on Saturday how it's going. If the calls are even a little bit shorter or less frustrating, I'll consider that progress.

Here are several other things Janice's mother could do:

- *Modeling how to deal with setbacks can certainly help.* Teens may not acknowledge listening to their parents, but they do. Talk out loud about your own perspective-taking on negative events. For example, "Oh well, I didn't get that promotion, but I did get a good performance review. There will be other opportunities."

Suggestions from Other Parents

- Help your teen test whether his perceptions are accurate. For example, ask, in a curious but not condescending way, "Did *everyone* do better than you?"
- Ask, "What would you tell a friend in this situation?"
- Ask, "Would you have felt that way if this happened last summer on vacation?" (implies that the current state of mind may be affecting perspective).
- Encourage looking at the evidence (for example, talk to people, investigate to check out your assumptions).
- Point out any possible "silver lining" of the current cloud (for example, mistakes allow us to learn).
- Point out that the world does not always judge us as harshly as we judge ourselves. Most people are too concerned about their own problems to spend much time evaluating others.
- Be a cheerleader rather than a judge of your child. (Criticism from others leads to self-criticism, and that *always* makes depression worse.)
- Focus on the problem rather than the problem child, and remind him what he is still doing well despite depression.
- Say, "You are not just your accomplishments."
- Look for opportunities for your teen to show himself he can do things. For example, encourage him to try a new game or activity you think he can manage, and then comment positively on how he did it for the first time with hardly any help from you.
- Praise even partial success ("You finished the race—that's great!"), no matter who actually won.
- Discourage your teen from rejecting imperfect peers (depressed teens often see others as "all good" or "all bad"), as they may become your friends if you get to know them and give them a chance.
- Create opportunities for discussion for the less verbal teen. For example: "If that had happened to me, I might have felt/thought…. Did you feel/think that or was it different for you?" (Provide him some possible thoughts and feelings to talk about, and he can choose which one to pick up on.) Or, for another example: "Many kids in that situation would feel hurt/embarrassed/worried….It wouldn't surprise me if you felt that way. How was it for you?"(Normalize vulnerable feelings and indicate it's OK to talk about them.)
- Encourage your child to keep a journal. Writing down what troubles you in a diary or journal isn't always just "wallowing." Some children use this to "get things off their chest" and find some relief in it. Prolonged time alone writing, however (just like prolonged time doing anything alone), can be a problem, as it reduces activity and increases depressive withdrawal.

- *Distracting depressed teens from their ruminations can help too.* Offer to play a favorite game, or point out an interesting show or activity.
- *If you know what the rumination is about, identify a recurring theme by saying, "It's one of those situations where X is happening again" and remind your teen what was helpful the last time this situation occurred.*
- *A helpful, empathic response to overly negative statements* (for example, "I can't do anything right") is, "I have days like that too." This implies that your teen is not alone in feeling down, and also that it is a temporary state (the next day may be different).

Some Don't's

- *Don't get trapped into an argument about how it "isn't really that bad,"* as this invalidates your child's suffering.
- *Don't offer overly general reassurances* such as, "It will be OK," or, "You'll be fine." These types of statements are sometimes calming for younger children, but they don't wash with teens. Remember: teens are able to think in terms of hypotheses and probabilities, so you will usually need to provide some logical reason why you believe "It will be OK" for the teen to accept that statement.
- *Don't assume that depression is the only thing distorting your teen's thinking.* Some teens also have distorted thinking related to anxiety or anger. We'll cover these areas later, but think in the meantime about how you would see yourself, others, and the future if you were either very anxious or very angry.
- *Don't burden your teen with your own doubts, insecurities, and (if you have them) mood problems.* Only share those personal feelings that you think would be helpful for him to know about. One parent summed it up nicely: "Be honest about how you feel, but be the parent!"

What Do You Say to the Teen Who Gets Stuck on "Why Me?"

Some depressed teens repeatedly ask, "Why me?" or similar questions indicating they are feeling sorry for themselves. Helpful things to say to them include: "It's unfair that you have this problem, but that means any accomplishment is all the greater when you do succeed." "Overcoming a disability like depression is work, but represents a real achievement." Both statements offer a nice combination of empathy and encouragement.

It is not helpful to say, "You're just feeling sorry for yourself" or "You're not the only one with problems." Although there may be truth to these statements, they invalidate the teen's feelings, making him feel worse and reducing the chances that he will share his feelings with you further.

What Do You Do If Your Teen's Distortions Border on Delusions?

A delusion is a way of thinking that is clearly out of touch with reality. In severe depression, some teens begin to think this way. An early sign is often the inability to distinguish between themselves (personal identity) and their depression. Attempts to correct their depressive thinking are met with, "This is just me! This is who I am!" At this stage, pointing out the teen's abilities that are separate from depression can be helpful. Send the message, "You are more than your depression," and indicate that you as a family are willing to "team up" with your teen's healthy abilities to fight depression (making the illness the villain, rather than your teen). Supporting your child's coping abilities that are *not* affected by depression is a great way to foster hope.

In some teens, this way of thinking can become more extreme, and the teen may claim, for example, that he is not part of normal society or part of his family (extreme alienation), that he was born to suffer or that he is being pursued by dark forces (delusions of persecution), that his brain or body is shrinking (extreme ideas about inadequacy/worthlessness), or that everything is so hopeless that he might as well be dead. Psychiatric intervention is more urgently needed in these teens, and they are unlikely to respond to the cognitive-behavioral approach described above without additional treatment (usually, medication and sometimes hospitalization). If your teen appears to be thinking in these more extreme ways, take him to an emergency department for an urgent assessment.

Exercise: Helping Your Teen with Depressed Thinking

List at the end of the chapter the ideas about changing depressed thinking (discussed above) that would be relatively easy for you to act on. Then, using these ideas, develop a L.E.A.P. plan for dealing with times when your teen engages in depressive thinking.

Key Points

Ways I can help my child overcome depressed thinking:

_____

_____

_____

_____

_____

_____

_____

_____

_____

Your L.E.A.P. plan response for this week is:

The situation: _____

_____

_____

_____

_____

Label your thoughts and feelings: _____

_____

_____

_____

_____

Empathize with your teen: _____

_____

_____

_____

_____

Explore ways to respond: _____

_____

_____

_____

_____

Apply alternative idea/plan: _____

_____

_____

_____

_____

Pick a follow-up time and plan ahead: _____

_____

_____

_____

_____

The Angry Depressed Child

When teens are depressed, other emotions may be affected as well. Besides sadness, anger and fear are the other basic negative emotions, and they often occur along with depression. Partly, this may relate to similar brain mechanisms involved in regulating various negative emotions. In teens, however, there are additional developmental reasons. For many teens who are trying to assert their independence, saying "I'm sad" makes them feel very vulnerable and threatened. It may be less threatening to express anger and say, for example, "You did this to me! That's so unfair!" Unfortunately, such expressions of anger are often interpreted by others as bad behavior, rather than signs of depression. That is why it is important to help depressed teens deal with their anger, and why anger is the focus of this chapter.

Marcy: *Marcy's depression was associated with very difficult behavior. Unlike some depressed teens, Marcy was hardly ever in her room. She began staying out later and later, then slept in until noon the next day. She met a new "boyfriend" online, and began to meet him at shopping malls. He was much older than she was, and had an extensive police record. She stopped calling her former friends from the debating team and the school band, and found a new crowd at school. Her new friends skipped class and experimented with various drugs. When her mother pointed out the risks of her behavior, Marcy just shrugged her shoulders. "So what do you care? I don't deserve any better."*

Progress Check

Did you try a L.E.A.P. plan based on last week's chapter on depressed thinking? Even if you didn't, did the ideas in the chapter help you understand where some of your depressed teen's statements may be coming from? What about the action tables or any other L.E.A.P. plans? Review what you would like to do with them this week.

If a L.E.A.P. plan is working but still challenging to do, persist with it another week. If it's working and becoming habitual, you're probably ready to focus on a new one. If it's not working, take a moment to reflect on reasons why, or talk with your spouse or a trusted friend about it. It may need some modification. Remember not to work on too many things at once. One or two plans are as many as most people can remember consistently.

Because Marcy had an aunt who had bipolar disorder (a condition with both depressed and extremely elated mood swings), she was initially assessed for this diagnosis. She did not have most of the features of this disorder, though, and a careful history revealed that not all of her behavior problems started with the depression. She had always been rather disrespectful toward her parents, frequently swearing at them, and did not do any chores at home. She was bright, though, and her academically oriented friends had helped her stay involved in several school activities. As long as she had kept this particular group of friends, everything appeared fine on the surface.

In the past, her parents had grudgingly accepted her defiance at home. Attempts to curtail it had never been successful. Marcy's father made excuses: "We did some foolish things when we were young too. She'll outgrow it." He was also consistently twenty minutes late for appointments. Marcy's mother had to be the "heavy" whenever a limit was set, only to hear her husband in the background saying, "Come on, Mary. It's not such a big deal." Marcy's mother arrived precisely on time for all appointments, but was frustrated with the lack of progress with Marcy's behavior and found herself frequently yelling at her daughter.

What Factors Other than Depression Were Causing Trouble for Marcy?

In this case, depression served to exacerbate a behavior problem that had been present for years. Although Marcy's temperament or genetics may have contributed to the bad behavior, her parents' inconsistent approach was a major factor in keeping it going. When teens get mixed messages from their parents, as Marcy did, they really get the message that the adults in the house are not in charge. If the adults are not in charge, teens feel free to make their own decisions and behave in whatever manner suits them. Teens have told us that, in the long run, this sort of inconsistency at home is confusing. After all, they are at a stage of development where they are yearning to learn how the world works and how they fit in. A clear, consistent model for this at home is reassuring to most teens.

Marcy's parents also inadvertently reinforced her negative behavior: her mother by yelling, and her father by undermining her mother's limits. If her father kept silent when Marcy's mother was setting a limit, and her mother was able to remain calm, Marcy would no longer receive as much negative attention for her actions and they would likely diminish over time.

In some families, inconsistency reflects differences in the way parents themselves were raised. For example, the rules may have been more lax in the father's family of origin than in the mother's. In other families, it reflects more serious marital problems. Either way, these issues should be addressed to allow parents to manage their teen's behavior as an effective team, rather than working at cross purposes.

Occasional differences of opinion about the teen may be resolved by parents gathering information and coming to a consensus, without professional involvement. More frequent differences about parenting issues may merit a discussion between the parents and a child and adolescent mental health professional. That professional can provide parenting advice and may also be able to determine whether there are differences that go beyond the area of parenting, and make a referral to a marital or family therapist if appropriate.

Why Do Depressed Teens Get Angry?

As discussed at the start of this chapter, a certain amount of irritability or anger can be part of depression, especially in teens, although Marcy's is an extreme case. It is therefore tempting to excuse the teen's anger with, "She can't help it. It's just her depression talking." Unfortunately, even if this attitude reduces conflict at home, the outside world will not be so forgiving. If your depressed teen is going to re-integrate into school and the world at large, she needs to keep that anger in check. Depression may make this task more difficult, but it's not impossible, especially if you begin the work at home.

Anger is the emotion that children and teens are least likely to change voluntarily. This is probably because anger doesn't feel so bad. It's a negative emotion, but it makes one feel strong, not vulnerable like fear or sadness. Therefore, external controls are often needed before children internalize anger management strategies. In other words, managing anger starts with behavior management. In the long run, managing anger has an added benefit: children who can't act out their frustrations are more likely to examine them, and find more appropriate ways of solving problems.

Anger can relate to cognitive distortions (for example, assuming that people who don't do what you want are deliberately malicious versus forgetful, uninformed, preoccupied with their own problems, etc.), but not always. Sometimes it's just a habitual way of getting attention or getting what you want. That's why behavior management focuses on decreasing attention and other "rewards" for anger.

What Can Parents Do about Angry Behaviors?

Some of you may have tried *1-2-3 Magic* or a similar time-out or attention withdrawal system when your children were younger. These systems involve warning the child when behavior is deteriorating, and if the behavior does not improve, giving the child a "time out" alone in her room or another specified location for a set period of time. The "time out" withdraws parental attention from the negative behavior, because parental attention is experienced as rewarding by most children. Thus, the child is no longer rewarded for negative behavior, and over time the behavior diminishes. Parents who have used this method often comment, "It doesn't work with teens anymore." Here are some alternatives:

- *Refer to the book SURVIVING YOUR ADOLESCENTS,* the follow-up to *1-2-3 MAGIC* written by the same author (Thomas Phelan, Ph.D; see the Bibliography at the end of this book).

- *Think about what time outs are really meant to accomplish.* They don't work because there is something magical about having children remain in their rooms. They work because they interrupt escalating arguments between parents and children, and they provide an "early warning system" that tells the child to try to calm her anger or stop misbehaving quickly, before a time out results. When they work well, time outs with at least one prior warning teach children anger control. When they don't work well, it's usually because one or both parents are having difficulty avoiding arguing or getting angry with the child. Arguments and anger constitute negative attention, and negative attention reinforces bad behavior. Children crave their parents' attention and will behave in ways that elicit that attention, even when the interaction is unpleasant.

- *"Less talk, less emotion" is an important rule of behavior management.* Even the teen who won't go to her room can be treated with "less talk, less emotion." You can stop talking and quietly carry on with your usual activities, or leave the room if your teen persists in trying to engage you in an argument.

- *Have a consequence for failing to contain anger in a reasonable time.* Small but significant consequences that can be administered frequently are ideal. For example, deducting 10 to 15 percent of her weekly allowance for each infraction often works better than telling your teen, "You're grounded for a month" (it's unenforceable). Thinking about consequences in advance and telling your teen what they are in a calm moment (assuming that all teens misbehave occasionally) is usually helpful, and avoids inconsistent or spur-of-the-moment penalties that are regretted later. It also reinforces the message that actions have consequences, and may act as a deterrent.

- **Whatever you do, do it consistently.** Make sure the response is the same each time, and that your partner is using the same response as you are. Persevere with a particular response for at least a month or two before switching to something else. Old habits die hard.

- **Don't let the threat of public embarrassment change what you do.** Better to look like a fool at the supermarket today than to be bailing your son or daughter out of jail in the future. Also, don't let pity for your child and her depression stop you from managing her behavior appropriately. In the long run, being firm is kinder than allowing depression to become an excuse for socially unacceptable behavior.

- **To avoid a lifetime of "allowance accounting," remember to pick your battles.** Some negative behaviors must have consequences (for example, breaking a wall in the house), some decrease with deliberate ignoring (for example, sarcastic remarks), and some fall in between. There are also behaviors that decrease in response to natural consequences (for example, getting angry with a peer who is bigger than your teen has consequences, and rarely persists for this reason). Only make an issue out of behaviors that are seriously "over the line" and/or would get your teen into trouble in the long run.

- **Identifying triggers that repeatedly lead to anger can be helpful.** In fact, some people describe the ABCs of behavior management as:
    1. Anticipation (behaviors that precede the angry outburst);
    2. Behavior (the outburst itself); and
    3. Consequences (others' reactions to the outburst).

Too often, we tend to focus exclusively on consequences (usually, punishments) and forget about the value of anticipation. Situations where anger flares up predictably are worth examining. Does your child or teen need a warning when such situations are coming up? In a calm moment, could you develop a plan with her to better handle such situations?

- **Offer to spend time alone with your teen.** She may outright refuse your offer and prefer to be with peers, but give her the message that you want to build this important relationship and allow her to choose the activity. Sometimes we get so focused on negative consequences for misbehavior that we forget about building on what goes well. Studies have shown that with younger children, more structured play time with parents decreases aggressive behavior. We wonder if tailoring this concept to teens might also decrease angry behaviors.

    For example, some depressed children or teens come home after a day of frustrations and put-downs (real or imagined) at school, and respond by beating a younger sibling or pet (the "kick the dog" behavior pattern). Why not anticipate trouble during the first hour after school? Make sure the teen has an activity or distraction available consistently at that time. Then, positively reinforce your teen for using the alternative activity or distraction rather than beating her sibling.

Common Misconceptions

Some parents think that behavior management means constantly punishing or timing out their teens. Nothing could be further from the truth. All behavior management should occur in the context of a caring, close relationship. It should be built on positive interactions with teens that include spending time together and praising pro-social and positive behaviors. Withdrawal of privileges or attention occurs only at times of misbehavior, and that leaves lots of time for closeness, talking, and affection. Furthermore, children who feel they can never please their parents because they always seem to be in trouble are likely to think, "Why bother trying to behave?" Commenting positively about how a child has *avoided* major misbehavior for a period of time, or praising more civil behavior is more powerful and effective than repeated consequences for negative behavior. For example, one boy we saw with daily tantrums was initially praised for just avoiding property damage in the course of his tantrums. In this case, it was a step in the right direction, and praising him for it worked.

There is also a common misconception that the "less talk, less emotion" rule means you can't explain things to your child. This is simply not true. Explanations, support, and encouragement are important for all children, but they need to occur when those involved are calm and not emotional. Make the time for them! Avoid talking *only* when your child is behaving inappropriately, to avoid reinforcing negative behavior. Conversely, talk more to your child at other times, to build a relationship based on healthy communication rather than arguments.

Parents tell us that some of their best "talk" times with their teens are when talk is not really being emphasized at all. In fact, they are busy doing things alongside each other (like chores, making supper, driving in the car) and not making eye contact. These times can prove more meaningful than either may have anticipated

Also remember that the occasional tantrum is not the end of the world. We once had a family ask for an anger management group for their fifteen-year-old son because, they said, "He has a complete meltdown two or even three times a year now!" Needless to say, we informed them they were luckier than most.

What If My Teen Wants Help with Managing Anger?

Good behavior management at home and at school is usually the first necessary step for containing anger at all ages. Once this is in place, some teens are willing to learn strategies for controlling anger themselves. "Anger management classes" in the absence of good behavior management are almost universally useless, though. The basic steps of anger management are outlined below, but if your teen is motivated to learn more *and* you are using consistent behavior management, pursue the classes.

Children or teens who want to learn to contain anger can often benefit from a two-step approach:

1. ***Disengage from the angry interaction.*** Disengagement can include leaving the room, taking a few deep breaths (without talking, just "breathe to 10"), or S.N.A.P. (snap fingers as a signal to "**S**top **N**ow **A**nd **P**lan"). All of these strategies are designed to curb impulsive action. Some children find it helpful to summon up a mental image as well (for example, seeing themselves as a particularly "cool" character they admire), or ask themselves, "Will this get me what I want?"

2. ***Think about alternative ways of dealing with the situation.*** Think about times when you have been angry yourself, to better understand the angry teen. Cognitively, angry people of all ages tend to see themselves as unfairly victimized, and other people as deliberately malicious. By going into situations with this attitude, they invite hostility from others. Because the assumptions underlying anger (especially those concerning other people) are similar to those of depression, anger and depression often go together. They are even more closely linked in teens than adults.

For teens, it sometimes helps to label an infuriating situation as "a situation where things didn't go quite as you thought they were supposed to" or "a situation where things seemed unfair," rather than focusing on the people involved. A situation can be managed better the next time (especially if the teen is willing to plan ahead for it); blaming others usually fuels thoughts of revenge.

The angry person may also struggle to take responsibility for the problem: "He made me do it" is a common excuse for fighting. Gently remind your teen that nobody can *make* you do things, but many people lose their cool from time to time. Then, focus on how to stay cool. **Most importantly, don't show anger back!**

Some further advice for parents of angry children can be found in *The Explosive Child* by Ross Greene, and older teens (if interested) may benefit from reading the chapter on anger in *Feeling Good* by David Burns (both listed in the Bibliography). If you have trouble managing anger yourself, it may also be worth a look. Losing one's temper is not a fault unique to teens. Burns helps people identify "cool thoughts" to counteract the "hot" ones—for example, "He did it on purpose," "It's so unfair," "They're picking on me," "It's wrong to act that way (and I have to make them stop)". In more serious aggression, medication is sometimes used.

What about Marcy?

Marcy's mother was faced with repeated curfew violations. When she demanded to know where Marcy had been, she got the angry response, "What do you care? You're just embarrassed that your daughter isn't Little Miss Perfect anymore." Rather than getting angry at Marcy and at her husband's unsupportive attitude, Marcy's mother began using the L.E.A.P. plan:

Label thoughts and emotions: I admit it *embarrassed* me when Marcy first began hanging around with her current friends, but that was a while ago. What I really feel now is *helpless*. I can't stop her staying out until all hours and getting into all sorts of trouble, and my husband doesn't seem to think there's anything wrong with this. It's a different world from when he and I grew up. Marcy is taking real risks, and I'm *afraid* for her! That's probably why I sound so desperate and shrill when I admonish her for being late.

Empathize with your teen: She knows the risks, but is taking them anyway. She doesn't care for herself enough to be safe. Someone has to show her she is worthy of care!

Explore ways to respond: Maybe I need to tell her I care more, rather than just nagging at her for disobeying. If I do that, though, I have to pick a time when she's not breaking the rules, or else I'd be rewarding rule-breaking! First thing in the morning might work. She hasn't done anything worthy of scolding at that point. When she does disobey, I need to show her I care again. Caring in that instance means risking her anger in order to protect her. That will be tough, as she's used to a fair bit of freedom at this point. I'll have to tighten the rules and stick to them. She shouldn't go out at all after school until she can respect herself! If she reacts badly and her father doesn't help, I might have to get some help from outside the family. If she gets violent, I might even have to involve the police! On the other hand, maybe it won't be so bad, and she can gradually earn back some freedoms as she shows she can handle them.

Apply an alternate idea/plan: Every morning, I'll tell Marcy that I love her and that she is important to me. I will get my friend Liz to pick her up from school every day and take her to a tutoring service to catch up on academic work. I'll pick her up from there, and she can have some TV or computer time at home to relax. She'll still be allowed time out with her friends on the weekends as long as she hasn't skipped any classes that week.

Pick a follow up time and plan ahead: I'll tell my husband the plan and ask him not to interfere. I can't expect his help, but he'll probably let me "do my thing" to keep the peace. I'll tell Marcy the new rules and how I hope they will help her. I won't look for her agreement either, but indicate that we will give this a try for two weeks and then talk to each other and the doctor about how it's going.

Exercise: Managing Anger

What types of situations make your teen really angry? How have you tried to help her deal with anger? Have you tried to set limits on her behavior? Work on a L.E.A.P. plan for an angry or difficult-to-manage behavior for your teen. Try it out this week.

Key Points

- Anticipate times of trouble.
- Pick your battles.
- Be consistent.
- Less talk, less emotion when behavior is inappropriate.
- Offer to spend time doing a favorite activity when your teen is *not* misbehaving.
- Use small, planned, consistent consequences.
- Praise abstinence from the worst misbehavior.
- Encourage your child to use a "disengage and think" strategy.
- Label the situation as problematic, rather than the person.
- Encourage your child to "think cool."

Your L.E.A.P. plan response for this week is:

The situation: _____

_____

_____

_____

_____

Label your thoughts and feelings: _____

_____

_____

_____

_____

Empathize with your teen: _____

_____

_____

_____

_____

Explore ways to respond: _____

_____

_____

_____

_____

Apply alternative idea/plan: _____

_____

_____

_____

Pick a follow-up time and plan ahead: _____

_____

_____

_____

Anxiety and Depression

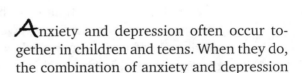

Anxiety and depression often occur together in children and teens. When they do, the combination of anxiety and depression results in more severe impairment than either one alone. The key to overcoming both problems is to improve overall functioning as well as to reduce anxious and depressive symptoms. This chapter focuses on helping teens reduce anxious symptoms.

Tammy: *While she was recovering from a serious depressive episode, Tammy went with her family to a fair. Behind one of the booths at the fair, she noticed a homeless man lying on the ground. When she pointed him out to her brother, the man opened his eyes, stared directly at Tammy, and angrily grabbed her arm, trying to pull her behind the booth. With her brother's help, Tammy was able to get away, and security guards arrived quickly to help. Nevertheless, from that day on Tammy was convinced she could not return to a normal life. She became housebound with anxiety, unable to walk on the sidewalk "in case someone attacks me." She had nightmares about the attack, was constantly tense and on edge during the day, and experienced a return of all her depressive symptoms.*

Tammy's story is, in some ways, a story of unfortunate coincidence. The assault she experienced would have been less likely to result in ongoing post-traumatic symptoms if she had not already been depressed, and the depression would have been more likely to fully resolve if she had not experienced the traumatic event. Sadly, coincidences like this do occur. Moreover, many teens experience concurrent anxiety and mood problems for other reasons. Often, depression follows prolonged anxiety problems, as teens become discouraged and hopeless about their inability to cope with anxiety. Some teens experience anxiety or panic attacks only when they are depressed. Whatever the reason, co-occurring anxiety and depression require a coordinated plan to address both conditions. We've already discussed some aspects of treatment for depression, but will now use Tammy's story to illustrate how concurrent anxiety might be addressed.

What Is Anxiety?

Anxiety is unrealistic or exaggerated fear. For example, if a large animal is chasing you in the woods and you are afraid of being hurt, that is a realistic fear. If the sight of a cocker spaniel on a leash makes you run away in terror, you are experiencing anxiety. Cocker spaniels can bite, but the chances of serious injury, particularly when the animal is on a leash, are extremely slim. Therefore, the fear is exaggerated and constitutes anxiety.

Symptoms of anxiety are of three general types:
1. avoidance of feared situations (the behavioral part of anxiety),
2. physical sensations associated with the sympathetic nervous system (basically, the "fight or fight" response: racing heart, shortness of breath, dizziness, sweating, "butterflies") or with tension (headaches, tummy aches), and
3. distressing or excessive worries (the mental part of anxiety).

In Tammy's case, she avoided not only the fair grounds but also any location outside her home because of a fear of attack (the behavioral part of anxiety). Her nightmares and feelings of tension or being on edge were physical manifestations of anxiety. Her excessive fear of being attacked was an ongoing worry (the mental part of anxiety).

Although all anxiety is characterized by the behavioral, physical, and mental components listed above, specific anxiety disorders have also been described. In an anxiety disorder, certain aspects of anxiety predominate and interfere with daily functioning. Teens who are depressed are sometimes diagnosed with these disorders, although an anxiety disorder should really not be diagnosed if the anxiety symptoms are clearly secondary to depression. In the event that your teen is diagnosed with one of these disorders, they will now be briefly described.

Types of Anxiety Disorders

Common anxiety disorders include:
- specific phobias (for example, of certain animals, of blood, or of enclosed spaces),

- social phobia,
- panic disorder,
- generalized anxiety disorder,
- obsessive compulsive disorder (OCD), and
- post-traumatic stress disorder (PTSD).

In the phobias, behavioral aspects of anxiety predominate and the person consistently avoids the situation(s) they fear. Social phobia can be particularly debilitating, as people with this disorder avoid many social situations for fear of embarrassment and can become quite isolated.

In panic disorder, the physical aspect of anxiety predominates. People suffering from panic disorder have repeated, intense episodes of shortness of breath, dizziness, and other anxiety symptoms. These episodes interfere with daily life, and eventually the fear of having them can result in avoidance of many situations.

In generalized anxiety disorder, worries (the mental aspect of anxiety) predominate. People with this disorder are always "living in the future," anxiously anticipating potential disasters. Obsessive compulsive disorder is different from other anxiety disorders, in that people with OCD are plagued by intrusive thoughts *not* related to worry, but feel compelled to do certain actions (termed compulsions) repeatedly in response to these thoughts.

Finally, post-traumatic stress disorder, Tammy's condition, is characterized by having all three types of anxiety symptoms (behavioral, physical, and mental) following a particularly frightening event.

Avoidance

Avoidance of feared situations reduces anxiety initially, but makes it worse in the long run. For example, a child with social phobia may avoid making telephone calls, fearing that he will become embarrassed or "tongue-tied" during the call. For similar reasons, he may also avoid picking up the telephone when it rings. The more the telephone is avoided, however, the more frightening the prospect of making a call becomes. As avoidance continues, conversation skills are lost, making it even harder to change. Without intervention, the problem becomes self-perpetuating.

For younger children, one of us (KM) has written a parenting book on helping with anxiety symptoms and overcoming avoidance. It is called *Keys to Parenting Your Anxious Child* (see Bibliography). The same principles used with young children can be adapted to teens. Basically, the teen must face each feared situation, starting with the easiest and working up to the most difficult, in order to desensitize to the fear.

Just like younger children, teens benefit from encouragement, praise, and positive reinforcement when trying to face a fear. Unlike younger children, however, teens' reinforcements for progress tend to be different. (Money or a special privilege may motivate teens, whereas stickers, prizes, or special time with a parent motivates younger children; praise is appropriate for all age groups.) You probably know better than anyone else what motivates your child or teen! To encourage desensitization:

- *Help your teen approach the situation in gradual steps with positive reinforcement for every little step.* In Tammy's case, several "levels" could be developed to overcome her avoidance. The first level would consist of spending time on her front porch, the second of venturing into the garden, the third of standing on the sidewalk, and so on. She should spend at least half an hour a day practicing leaving the house (a minimum for desensitization), with graduated rewards for progressing to higher "levels." For the socially anxious child mentioned above who won't talk on the telephone, a different system of levels would apply. In this case, having someone else place the call (to a familiar, non-threatening person previously informed of the exercise) and then asking the child to provide a whispered, one-word response to a specific question on the telephone may be the first step. You need to use the same principle: gradual approximations. Setting up appropriate desensitization systems is a whole course (or book) in itself.
- *Gradually withdrawing support in a situation can also be a step.* For example, one mother of a young teen encouraged her daughter to travel on the public transit system to her appointments by accompanying her at gradually increasing distances until they were essentially traveling independently. She praised this "grown up" behavior throughout the process (no other reward was needed).
- *Relaxation and coping self-talk* (see below) can also help children go into avoided situations with less fear.
- Because going into a feared situation is an activity, you may also wish to *review the earlier chapter on motivating teens to engage in activities.*

Physical Symptoms

Panic attacks that come "out of the blue" (with no apparent trigger) and are frequent usually require either medication or a separate course of cognitive-behavioral therapy that targets panic. Anxiety symptoms that are triggered by worries or by certain situations, however, often improve with relatively simple relaxation techniques. These techniques also help reduce physical tension and tension-related pain. Doing them at bedtime often improves sleep. Obviously, you can't get someone to relax by ordering them to do so. In fact, saying "Relax!" usually makes people more tense. Try the relaxed breathing technique described in Chapter 5 as a "healthy habit." Doing this is truly relaxing.

Tensing and relaxing the muscles, one at a time, slowly, is another common technique. You can start at the toes, working up the legs and torso to the head, and then from the shoulders down to the hands and fingers. The order is not important, as long as all the main areas of the body are covered. Some people combine relaxed breathing or muscle relaxation with soothing mental imagery such as imagining lying on a beach and hearing the surf on the sand. Whatever your teen finds calming and is able to incorporate into his daily life is usually best. Give it a couple of weeks to work, though, as people relax more deeply with daily practice.

How Do You Get Children and Teens to Do Relaxation?

- *Modeling relaxation* often helps (you might find you enjoy it!). For example, you might come home from work and do some relaxation before dinner.
- *Doing relaxation together* (another variation on modeling) also makes it seem more acceptable to teens.
- *Doing relaxation as part of another discipline* is another nice option. (Karate, yoga, voice training, and certain sports all involve diaphragmatic breathing.)
- Some teens prefer *relaxation tapes that they can use independently.* Eli Bay (see Bibliography) has several to choose from. Encourage your teen to use a tape that contains an actual exercise, though. Soft music with nature sounds in the background doesn't always have the same beneficial effect.
- The *good health habits* we discussed earlier also promote relaxation (especially regular exercise and avoiding caffeine).

If your child has physical pain (headache, stomachache) that may have a psychological component, resist the urge to say, "It's all in your head," or, "It's just nerves." These types of pain feel real, despite their psychosomatic origin. First, check with you child's doctor to rule out a physical cause. Then, acknowledge that the pain is real, but suggest that it is unlikely to get worse with relaxation, and it might improve (though you shouldn't expect the pain to disappear completely). Abdominal crunches (a variation on muscle relaxation), for example, are often helpful with tummy pain.

Worries

Depressed children have distorted ways of seeing the future, themselves, and others. Do you remember the depressive triad (worthless self, uncaring world, hopeless future)? Now, how would you see the future, yourself, and the world if you were anxious? Probably, you would see a weak self, a dangerous world, and an uncertain future. Now, imagine how you would see things if you were both depressed and anxious. This would be quite a load on your mind! In Tammy's case, her view that she risked attack just by leaving the house was an anxious distortion. The danger outside her home was overestimated in this case.

All of the same ideas we discussed for depressive distortions apply to anxious ones too:

- *Help your child examine the evidence for or against the worry.* (Usually, things aren't nearly as dangerous as what we anticipate.)

- *Because worries often concern uncertain future events, you may have to look at probabilities as well.* (What are the chances this will happen? What else could happen? What are the chances of that?)
- *Try to emphasize personal competence.* (Can you do anything to reduce the risk? If not, can you do anything to limit the worry time so worries don't control your life?)
- *See if your teen can identify the worried state* (for example, before bed is a common time when worries take hold). If so, encourage "catching yourself worrying" and then either doing something distracting or writing down the worry. Although it's not easy, some teens can learn to write down bedtime worries and then let them go until the morning. Also, if every worry must be written down, the activity becomes fatiguing and eventually induces sleep.
- At a calm time, you may want to **discuss the pros and cons of worrying.** (For example, occasionally, people can find new solutions to a problem after worrying about it, but more often worrying just causes distress and wastes time, so on balance it's not worth it.)
- *Some teens will agree to a "worry time," which is usually a few minutes to half an hour where they can worry as much as they want.* The deal is, however, that you must postpone worries to your "worry time" the rest of the day.
- *Remember to also model good coping with anxiety-provoking situations.* This is particularly helpful if your teen doesn't voice his worries to you. For example, if you are driving in snowy conditions, you could say, "This is not good. It's really starting to come down heavily, but then I've driven in this kind of weather before. I can slow down and still get to where I'm going. I can always pull over if it gets worse." Interestingly, you are not modeling fearlessness, but coping well despite your fears. Thus, you are modeling both acknowledging worry and good coping, thereby encouraging your teen to discuss worried feelings.

Does Anxiety or Depression Get Treated First?

In children and teens who struggle with both conditions, priorities need to be set. This avoids having them work on too many things at once, which could result in failure and discouragement. Usually, the first priority is the problem that is interfering with day-to-day life the most.

Tammy (continued): *In Tammy's case, her inability to leave the house was a big problem. Desensitizing her to going outdoors was the first treatment goal. While* *working on this, however, a psychotherapist helped her talk about the traumatic event she had just experienced, to help her put it into perspective. Over time, this reduced her nightmares, allowing for better sleep. Once she was sleeping better and able to leave the house, the treatment focus switched back to overcoming depression and returning to school. Throughout treatment, she obtained relief from both her anxiety symptoms and her depression by taking an antidepressant medication.*

Even with this thoughtful plan and ongoing professional involvement, Tammy's recovery was not entirely smooth. Returning to school became a major stumbling block. Tammy had been away from school for three months, and was very worried about going back. She no longer feared being attacked, but felt very worried about the amount of work she would have to catch up on, and about dealing with friends' reactions to her absence. The first worry was addressed through a discussion with her teacher who, fortunately, was sympathetic and agreed to modify Tammy's workload. The second worry was more difficult to reassure. "What do I tell my friends about why I was away? Everybody is going to be asking me 1001 questions!" Tammy exclaimed.

Tammy's parents developed a L.E.A.P. plan together to address her concerns about explaining her absence to her classmates and friends:

Label thoughts and feelings: Tammy's parents both felt *pressured* about getting her back to school as soon as possible. Just when they thought things were progressing and Tammy was dealing with her fears of being attacked, she seemed to backslide with these school worries. They began to despair: "If it's not one thing, it's another." By labeling their *disappointment* and putting it into perspective, however, they were able to encourage each other to stay hopeful.

Empathize with your teen: Labeling their own overwhelmed feelings helped Tammy's parents empathize with her. "After all, we are just seeing this unfold from the sidelines...she's living it!" her father volunteered.

Is It Anxiety or Depression?

Sometimes, it is difficult to tell anxiety and depression apart. Certainly the physical symptoms of anxiety can be quite striking, but (as discussed above) they are not characteristic of all anxiety problems. Avoidance is thought to be anxiety-related, but depressed teens with low energy levels can avoid many situations as well. Thinking tends to be more hopeless and self-deprecating in depression, and more uncertain or focused on danger in anxiety, but there are similarities in these thinking styles. For example, "I know I'll just end up looking like a fool if I try to give my presentation in Biology" sounds hopeless, but could also represent social anxiety.

Overall, it is therefore probably best to leave the diagnosing to the professionals, and instead ask yourself questions like: "What symptoms are getting in the way the most for my teen?" "What thoughts/feelings/behaviors are stopping my teen from participating in what others his age enjoy?" Answers to these questions will allow you to work with your teen and the professionals to prioritize what areas need to be addressed first, as shown below in relation to Tammy.

"Tammy's had so much to overcome, it's amazing she's still hanging in there. With a bit of encouragement, I'll bet she can deal with this too."

Explore ways to respond: Tammy's parents explored ideas for helping her deal with her peers' questions. "I was sick, but I'm better now," "I was really stressed and couldn't handle school for a while," or simply, "I'd rather not get into it. What are you guys doing?" were some possible responses they thought Tammy could use. They thought getting Tammy to ask her friends some questions might help take some of the focus off her. They also wondered about involving her teacher in a supportive way, but weren't sure if that would embarrass her more. They thought reviewing relaxation exercises with Tammy might help as well.

Apply alternative ideas/plan: Tammy's parents empathized with her reluctance to go back, and praised her for her progress to date, pointing out all the positive steps she had taken since she was attacked. They framed a return to school as a big step, but one that could be broken down into smaller steps. The step of dealing with the academic load had already been taken. Starting out with attending half days (rather than full days) was another way of breaking it into small steps.

Dealing with the other teens was a similar small step. They role played possible scenarios (even the worst case ones) and developed some scripted responses with Tammy to deal with her friends' questions and take the focus off herself. With her permission, they also informed her homeroom teacher about this concern, so she would have at least one sympathetic person to turn to if she encountered problems her first few days back at school. They also reviewed relaxation breathing, reminding Tammy that she could do this anytime, anywhere without anyone noticing.

Pick a follow up time and plan ahead: Tammy's parents agreed to evaluate this plan daily for the first week of school, focusing on what went well and what remained a challenge. To maintain an encouraging attitude, Tammy's parents agreed to praise her efforts and successes, and refrain from commenting on any setbacks. Assuming at least some success the first week of school, they agreed to evaluate the plan at least weekly after that.

Exercise: Dealing with Anxious Situations

What anxieties has your child faced? How have you tried to help? Have you dealt with anxieties yourself? What did you find helpful? See if you can use your own experience to develop a L.E.A.P. plan for an anxious situation your teen is finding difficult.

Key Points

- For overcoming avoidance, encourage your child to gradually face the feared situation one step at a time.
- For physical symptoms of anxiety, encourage relaxed breathing and muscle relaxation, as well as generally good health habits.
- "The more the merrier" when it comes to relaxation. Do it together.
- Model how you cope with anxiety-provoking situations.
- Examine the evidence and the probabilities for worries.
- Emphasize what your child can do to reduce the risk of what is feared or reduce the worry time.

Your L.E.A.P. plan response for this week is:

The situation: _____
_____
_____
_____
_____

Label your thoughts and feelings: _____
_____
_____
_____
_____

Empathize with your teen: _____
_____
_____
_____
_____

Explore ways to respond: _____
_____
_____
_____
_____

Apply alternative idea/plan: _____
_____
_____
_____
_____

Pick a follow-up time and plan ahead: _____
_____
_____
_____
_____

Depression and the Family (Part 1)

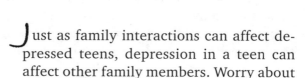

Just as family interactions can affect depressed teens, depression in a teen can affect other family members. Worry about having an ill child, concern about social stigma, and feelings of being neglected by your partner (if he or she is more involved in the teen's care) are common feelings among parents. Concerns about whether or not your actions or your genes "caused" your teen's depression can be a further burden. Unfortunately, all of these feelings occur at a time when the need for parents to work as a team is higher than ever. Needless to say, preexisting family tensions often get worse when a teen is depressed. If needed, don't be shy about asking for help outside the family to deal with these.

Siblings can also suffer when a child or teen is depressed. They may feel neglected, feel guilty or responsible for the child's depression (especially if their relationship with the child was not great before the depression), feel envious of the extra attention given to the depressed child, or feel concerned about the stigma of having a "crazy" family member. Siblings may also miss the good times they used to have when the child was healthy. They may have difficulty understanding depression as well. Younger siblings sometimes fear they might "catch" depression when the problem is described as an illness. Older siblings who have gone through some difficult times themselves may be annoyed at the depressed teen's inability to cope, seeing it as weakness. Too often, we

Progress Check

Did you remember to follow up on your L.E.A.P. plan(s)? Take a moment to review progress now.

fail to take the time to talk to siblings and explore their thoughts and feelings about the depressed teen.

Today, we will begin to talk about depression and families. If you read the books, it sounds as if there are many types of families that are prone to having depressed children, and even more theories to account for this. We will discuss the theories we believe are more valid and also explore some ways that you can help your family better cope with the effects of depression.

Family Dynamics and Depression

Probably the best-studied family problems in relation to depressed teens are:

1. "expressed emotion" (basically, a tendency for family members to criticize each other a lot), and
2. "affectionless control" (parenting characterized by close monitoring of children and emphasis on obedience, but little affection).

Although several studies have identified these problems in families, bear in mind that many of these studies relied on the descriptions provided by depressed individuals. Depressed individuals, as we have discussed, can have cognitive distortions that affect their perceptions of themselves and others, including family members. Thus, depressed individuals may be very sensitive to signs of criticism, rejection, or attempts to control them. Awareness of this sensitivity, however, can help you respond to your teen with greater empathy, and thus offer genuine support.

Family "Circles"

An important general principle of family dynamics is that families don't cause depression, and depressed children don't cause family problems. "Causes" in families tend to be circles. If you do something that upsets another family member, she will respond by doing something that upsets you, and before you know it, nobody knows who started it, and "who started it" becomes the least of concerns. The problems lie in the interactions, rather than in any one person. Therefore, look for *patterns* that cause trouble, rather than people to blame.

One way to better understand relationships, and, specifically, the interactions that occur between people that can cause problems, is to visually map out the interactions. Karl Tomm (1987) from the University of Calgary developed circular pattern diagrams to help therapists and families better understand the mutual influence of one person's thoughts, feelings, and behavior on that of the other. Sometimes patterns of interaction are complementary and mutually helpful. Sometimes the patterns are problematic and family members feel stuck and want to change them. (See Figure 1.)

Figure 1: "A Circular Pattern"

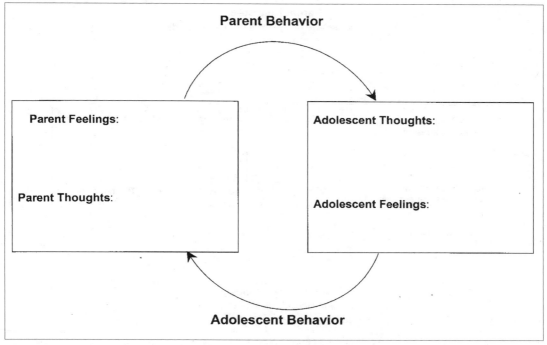

Parent Behavior

Parent Feelings:

Parent Thoughts:

Adolescent Thoughts:

Adolescent Feelings:

Adolescent Behavior

Example: _____

Child and adolescent psychiatrist Dr. Mark Sanford and nurse Dr. Lynn McCleary developed four patterns that commonly occur in interactions between parents and their depressed teens. They are not exclusive to families with depression, nor do all families of depressed teens necessarily fall into any one of them. In fact, we encourage parents to take the concepts of circular pattern diagrams and develop their own individualized patterns—one(s) that they can map out and then work towards changing.

Consider these four common circular patterns of interaction that occur between parents and their depressed teens:

1. In the **reassure-cling pattern** (see Figure 2 on the next page), excessive parental reassurance undermines the adolescent's self-confidence, resulting in clinging, and the clingy adolescent in turn makes the parent feel worried and protective, resulting in even more reassurance.

2. In the **withdraw-cling pattern** (see Figure 3 on the next page), the parent withdraws emotionally from the adolescent, leaving her feeling unsupported and worried about being unable to cope, prompting clinging behavior, which makes the parent feel burdened and even more inclined to withdraw.

3. In the **pursue-withdraw pattern** (see Figure 4 on page 117), the parent repeatedly tries to elicit communication from the

Figure 2: "The Reassure-Cling Pattern"

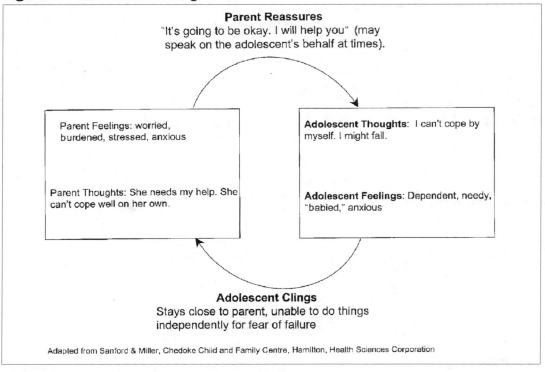

Parent Reassures
"It's going to be okay. I will help you" (may speak on the adolescent's behalf at times).

Parent Feelings: worried, burdened, stressed, anxious

Parent Thoughts: She needs my help. She can't cope well on her own.

Adolescent Thoughts: I can't cope by myself. I might fail.

Adolescent Feelings: Dependent, needy, "babied," anxious

Adolescent Clings
Stays close to parent, unable to do things independently for fear of failure

Adapted from Sanford & Miller, Chedoke Child and Family Centre, Hamilton, Health Sciences Corporation

Figure 3: "The Withdraw-Cling Pattern"

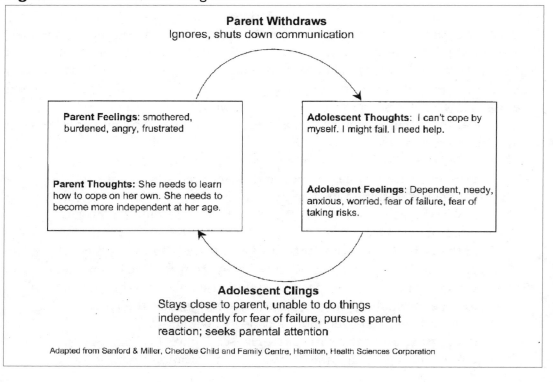

Parent Withdraws
Ignores, shuts down communication

Parent Feelings: smothered, burdened, angry, frustrated

Parent Thoughts: She needs to learn how to cope on her own. She needs to become more independent at her age.

Adolescent Thoughts: I can't cope by myself. I might fail. I need help.

Adolescent Feelings: Dependent, needy, anxious, worried, fear of failure, fear of taking risks.

Adolescent Clings
Stays close to parent, unable to do things independently for fear of failure, pursues parent reaction; seeks parental attention

Adapted from Sanford & Miller, Chedoke Child and Family Centre, Hamilton, Health Sciences Corporation

Figure 4: "The Pursue-Withdraw Pattern"

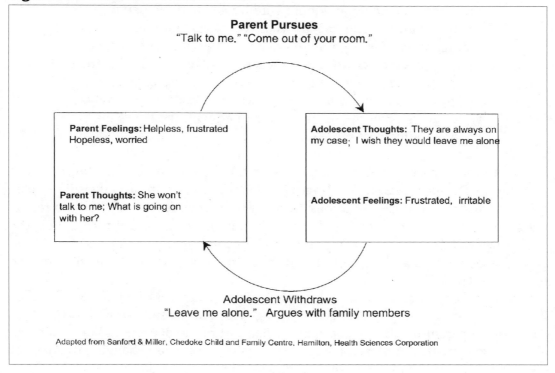

Parent Pursues
"Talk to me." "Come out of your room."

Parent Feelings: Helpless, frustrated Hopeless, worried

Parent Thoughts: She won't talk to me; What is going on with her?

Adolescent Thoughts: They are always on my case; I wish they would leave me alone

Adolescent Feelings: Frustrated, irritable

Adolescent Withdraws
"Leave me alone." Argues with family members

Adapted from Sanford & Miller, Chedoke Child and Family Centre, Hamilton, Health Sciences Corporation

Figure 5: "The Criticize-Withdraw Pattern"

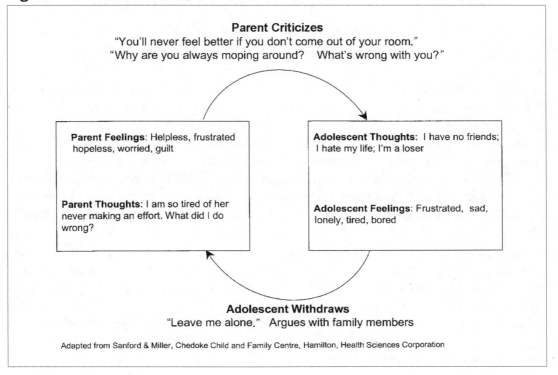

Parent Criticizes
"You'll never feel better if you don't come out of your room."
"Why are you always moping around? What's wrong with you?"

Parent Feelings: Helpless, frustrated hopeless, worried, guilt

Parent Thoughts: I am so tired of her never making an effort. What did I do wrong?

Adolescent Thoughts: I have no friends; I hate my life; I'm a loser

Adolescent Feelings: Frustrated, sad, lonely, tired, bored

Adolescent Withdraws
"Leave me alone." Argues with family members

Adapted from Sanford & Miller, Chedoke Child and Family Centre, Hamilton, Health Sciences Corporation adolescent, the adolescent feels the parent is being intrusive and responds with anger and more withdrawal, and the parent is frustrated and worried about what the adolescent might be hiding, prompting even more attempts to elicit communication.

4. In the **criticize-withdraw pattern** (see Figure 5 on the previous page), the parent criticizes the adolescent, exacerbating feelings of inadequacy in the teen, who responds by passively withdrawing, and the parent is frustrated with the teen's inactivity, prompting even more criticism.

Note that we described these patterns starting with the parent, but they can be described equally well as starting with the adolescent. In fact, it's silly to ask, "Who started it?" in these situations. The key to change is for somebody to recognize the pattern and change his or her own part in it. More often than not, the parent has to start to map it out and consider changing aspects of her part of the circle, as depression and immaturity make it more difficult for the teen to realize her role in what is happening.

Take a moment to think about how each of these patterns of interaction could be interrupted and eventually changed, starting with the parent's response. (Hint: in each case, a parent needs to explore his or her part of the pattern and determine an alternative, empathic approach based on the child's needs. By changing one part of the cycle, the parent influences the entire pattern of interaction.)

Mapping Out a Pattern of Interaction between Yourself and Your Teen

Take a blank circular pattern diagram (see Figure 1) and write down one of your teen's behaviors (at the very top) that is problematic for you in a particular situation. Start with something specific, not general. Then ask yourself (and write down in the Parent Thought section) what your thoughts are as you observe and experience your teen's behavior. Next, when you have those thoughts, what do you feel? Write it down. Next, at the bottom of the circle, write down what you specifically do when you experience her behavior, think your thoughts, and feel your feelings.

The next part requires some guessing on your part. When your teen experiences your behavior, what do you think she thinks? What do you think she feels? Write your ideas down in the allocated sections of the circle. It is likely then that her behavior (the one you initially listed) will make more sense to you as you understand how she may be responding to your behavior. It is important to note that you are not necessarily right or wrong, but that your behavior is one of the many components on the circle that could be changed. When one part of the circle changes, it is likely that other parts will change as well. The exercise of mapping out the patterns is simply a way to generate new ideas and possible solutions to stuck patterns between people. In our work, we also apply circular pattern diagrams to other relationships, such as couples', siblings', and friends' relationships.

Bill: *Bill had a cordial but distant relationship with his parents. They explained, "We love our son dearly, but we just can't figure him out! He keeps everything inside." Bill had a large "Do Not Disturb" sign on his bedroom door. Inquiries from the other side were met with, "Whaddya want?" His usual response to specific questions was a grunt. Bill's parents responded with increasing concern.*

"What's he hiding in there? You don't suppose he's on drugs?" his mother wondered. When questions got her nowhere, she began going through his room periodically "to clean." She cleaned thoroughly: under the furniture, inside the drawers, even between the mattresses. Bill resented the rather obvious intrusion on his privacy. "Tell me the day you want to clean and I'll do it myself!" he protested. Bill's mother agreed, but soon began "losing things" and having to search for them in his room. Bill responded by purchasing a small combination safe and keeping his most personal possessions locked up there.

His mother was beside herself with worry, and turned to her husband. "Don't look at me. I don't know how those things work!" said Bill's father. "Let's get some advice on this."

Bill and his mother illustrate the pursue-withdraw pattern of parent-child interaction. The more Bill's mother pursued information about him, the more he withdrew and guarded his privacy in an escalating cycle. Fortunately, Bill's family agreed with the father's suggestion, and all were seen in family therapy with good results. Without help, the pattern in Bill's family might well have intensified, and, with increasing frustration on both sides, could have evolved into the criticize-withdraw pattern as well (a common progression). Note also that the withdraw-cling pattern is really pursue-withdraw in reverse: the parent withdraws emotionally instead of the child.

Working out Differences between Parents in Parent-Teen Patterns

Not uncommonly, the mother and father interact differently with their teen. This may not be a major problem in some families as both parents and teens learn to navigate small differences. However, one of the most common difficulties involves teens who respond to inconsistency between parents by teaming up with one parent against the other. Perhaps one parent is more sympathetic to the teen's problems while the other is more "no nonsense," leading to a closer bond with the first parent. Whatever the reason, the result is that parents can no longer work as a team to help the teen. In these situations, any marital difficulties that exist are likely to be exacerbated. Look back at the example of Marcy (in Chapter 7) to see an illustration of this type of family difficulty.

Another common problem occurs when one parent simply cannot provide what the child or teen needs, and the other is minimally involved. In this case, it's a matter of showing the uninvolved parent how important he or she can be to the child or teen. Sometimes parents can discuss and solve this problem themselves, particularly if the less involved parent is given specific suggestions of what to do. For example, the more involved parent could say to their spouse something like, "Michael is really into chess these days, and you know so much more about that than I do. I think he'd love to play it with you once in a while." In other situations, when parents can't agree on the amount or quality of involvement with their teen, a mental health professional may be required to help each one (or both) develop the underdeveloped relationship.

> **Joe:** *Joe had always been shy and socially withdrawn, but was well-liked by his teachers because he worked hard at school. He had a good relationship with his mother, though he didn't confide in her about "personal stuff." In sixth grade, Joe's peers began to tease him more and he developed symptoms of depression. Joe responded well to psychotherapy, but still didn't have any friends. Joe's father attended his initial psychiatric assessment appointment, but was not involved in treatment because he was "not touchy-feely" (in his words). After talking to his wife (the more involved parent) about Joe's lack of social and physical activity, however, his Dad decided to provide Joe with baseball equipment and bring him to the park each day. Since the equipment was Joe's, the other children had to include Joe if they wanted to play a game. Joe came out of his shell quickly after that, and his mood improved further.*

What Happened in Bill's Family?

Before addressing possible unhealthy patterns in your own family, let's take another look at Bill's family. Although they sought family therapy, the basic ideas from that therapy can be summarized in a L.E.A.P. plan. Let's take the perspective of Bill's mother.

Label your thoughts and feelings: I am so *worried* about Bill's secrecy. What could he be hiding? I wish I could pry it out of him, but he won't talk to me. Searching his things and asking questions is getting me nowhere, and I'm kind of *embarrassed* about the excuses I've been making lately to get into his room.

Empathize with your teen: If I was a teenager and my mother was nosing around my room all the time, I might be reluctant to talk to her as well. I remember how self-conscious I was at that age, and how I valued my own space.

Explore ways to respond: Maybe I could make a deal with Bill to leave his room alone during the week if I can see it at least once on the weekend. After all, so far the worst things I've found in there are vile gym socks and moldy food. If he doesn't want to tell me everything, maybe we could at least agree to discuss important things like school progress, special events, and major decisions. He may appreciate my getting off his back regarding the minor stuff. Sharing some of my feelings with him may help too. Even if I just get an adolescent grunt in return, at least he'll know I'm willing to let my guard down and risk being open about certain things. He might open up to his father sometimes too, and I know my husband would let me know if he found out anything serious.

Apply alternative ideas/plan: I'll sit down with Bill and his father and propose to check Bill's room only once a week. I'll see if we can all agree to communicate about important things, but avoid prying if the other person doesn't want to discuss the issue. I'll try to model discussing my feelings, in hopes that Bill will follow suit.

Pick a follow up time plan ahead: I'll keep track of how many times a week I get angry accusations from Bill about not respecting his privacy, and how often I get really worried about him. If the numbers go down, nothing further may be needed. If not, or if Bill gives me a serious reason to worry, I'll try talking with my husband about it first, before trying to get the answers from Bill.

In this case, things didn't change overnight (old patterns are hard to change), but Bill did eventually talk more when he experienced his mother as less intrusive, and everyone was much more relaxed and less suspicious of each other after a few months.

What Are Some Obstacles to Changing Negative Patterns?

Some common obstacles include:

- *Poor "fit" in temperaments* (for example, athletic child in an intellectual family or vice versa; whiny, demanding child in a family that values independence and autonomy). While temperament cannot be changed, accepting a child's temperament, even when it seems to differ from yours and other family members', is within your control.
- *Having experienced less than optimal parenting yourself* (the old patterns come naturally, as they've been modeled for you a thousand times; the new patterns don't).
- *Problems in early attachment with this child* (for example, if she was the result of an unplanned pregnancy or born with medical problems). A child who has experienced attachment problems may exhibit more anxious behaviors, have difficulty with trust, and may be more likely to protest during times of transition. These may require psychotherapy for the parent so that he or she can respond to the child's special needs.
- *Personal mental health issues* (to be discussed more in the next chapter).

In this chapter, we have encouraged parents to think about interactions between themselves and their children or between other family members that they notice and would like to change. However, even though parents really try to do what is in the best interest of their child, sometimes certain choices seem good but can create difficulties in the long run. Common examples of this difficulty include:

- Being "buddies" with a teen can feel great, but complicates discipline.
- Searching her room for contraband may reassure you in the short term but diminishes trust in the relationship in the long-term.
- Providing for her every need or desire may make you feel like a loving parent, but doesn't help the teen grow up.

Nevertheless, to develop an effective L.E.A.P. plan for family problems, a thoughtful, empathic approach focused on the best interest of your child is exactly what's needed. Take a moment to think about what pattern within your family you would like to try to change. We have included a blank circular pattern (Figure 1) for you to use in mapping out a problematic pattern between you and your teen. Remember, though, it can be between any two family members!

Exercise: Changing Unhealthy Patterns

Most of the time it is difficult to see our part in a problem involving one or more other people. It is often easier to just see the other half of the circle, the part that isn't ours. Yet when parents closely examine their patterns, they often feel more able to shift them. By stepping into the shoes of their teen, they not only better understand and empathize with the teen, but they also see how they can positively influence their relationship with their teen.

What patterns in your family cause trouble? Do they fit any of the ones described, at least in the parent-child relationships? Are other family members such as siblings involved in unhealthy ways? For example, a sibling of a depressed teen may feel jealous of the attention the parents give the teen. The sibling may engage in negative cycles with the teen or with the parent around this issue. She may tease her sister for taking medication, which in turn may cause the depressed teen to think worse of herself, feel more isolated, and become angry and aggressive. This may in turn perpetuate a negative cycle between siblings. Let's further suppose that the parent gets involved in the sibling dispute, which provides negative attention to the sibling and possibly exacerbates the problematic cycle. Here we see how all three can become entangled in cycles, all in the name of the sibling vying for parental attention. By mapping out the cycle between the siblings, the parent would likely become more aware of the root of the sibling's teasing and choose to break the cycle by spending more time with the sibling rather than reinforcing the teasing by providing negative attention.

What can you do to start changing these patterns in your family?

1. Change your thoughts, feelings, and/or response to the child?
2. Involve another family member in a different way?

Write down your idea(s) on the next page, and pick one for a L.E.A.P. plan response.

Key Points

Depressed children do better with families where there is:
- Low conflict
- Low criticism
- High affection
- Reasonable limits
- Mutual respect
- Parents working as a team

To bring my family closer to this utopian ideal, the pattern(s) most in need of change is/are:

_____

_____

_____

_____

My role in starting this change will be:

_____

_____

_____

_____

Your L.E.A.P. plan response for this week is:

The situation: _____
_____
_____
_____
_____

Label your thoughts and feelings: _____
_____
_____
_____

Empathize with your teen: _____
_____
_____
_____

Explore ways to respond: _____
_____
_____
_____

Apply alternative idea/plan: _____
_____
_____
_____

Pick a follow-up time and plan ahead: _____
_____
_____
_____

Depression and the Family (Part 2)

According to the U.S. Surgeon General's Report on Mental Health, mood disorders are significant causes for disability worldwide. Approximately 25 percent of women and about 15 percent of men will be affected by depression and other related disorders such as substance abuse and anxiety in their lifetime. Many of these men and women are, of course, parents. So, there is a fair chance that you and/or your spouse may have been affected by depression at some time or are currently depressed.

There is a lot of research that has explored the impact of parental depression on children and the impact of depression on families as units. If you are positive that depression is not a problem for you or your spouse, skip this chapter and go on to Chapter 14. If neither you nor your spouse is currently depressed, review last week's L.E.A.P. plan on family interactions, and repeat if needed.

In this chapter we review a special situation in families of depressed children: what if you (the parent) are or have been depressed? It's not unusual, given the high heritability of mood problems. Amanda's story, below, is an example of how depression can become a recurring theme in a family:

Amanda: *Amanda was a straight "A" student, and loved it. Every term she came home with a report card full of superlative comments from her teachers. Her father*

Progress Check

How are your L.E.A.P. plans from previous weeks coming? Are there one or two responses that are starting to become routine, even when you don't think about it? If so, that's wonderful. If not, look back and repeat a L.E.A.P. response this week that you found valuable so far.

would take one look and beam, eager to show his friends in the neighborhood. Amanda's mother would smile too, but weakly. She suffered from recurrent bouts of depression. She often told Amanda about her childhood, about her unfulfilled dreams, and about all she had given up when she was forced to marry because she was pregnant with Amanda. Amanda listened and offered comfort. Around the house, Amanda tended to agree with everything her mother said, and would nod obediently as her mother stated, "We would like some classical music, please," and gestured towards the radio.

Amanda rarely socialized with her peers. "I'm too busy with my studies," was her usual explanation. Inside, she was painfully shy and terrified of social embarrassment. Occasionally, she made a friend at school, usually when another girl approached her to do an activity at recess, but she almost never saw peers outside of school.

When Amanda started high school, two things happened: first, it became increasingly difficult for her to obtain straight "A's." Second, Amanda felt increasingly uncomfortable agreeing with her mother about everything. As the "A's" diminished, so did her father's affection. He had thought Amanda could realize his childhood dreams of going to college. Now, he began to doubt this would happen. Amanda's mother, on the other hand, became increasingly irritating to her because she presented opinions as though they were facts, and would not consider alternative points of view. Rather than echoing her mother's views as she had in the past, Amanda began to respond with silence when she wasn't sure she agreed. Her mother interpreted this behavior as defiance, and responded by not speaking to her daughter for several hours at a time.

Increasingly, Amanda felt alone and sad at home. With no close friends to turn to, she tried to figure out her problems herself. Unfortunately, the more she thought about things, the more she doubted herself and her place in the world. She went back and forth between resenting her mother for using her as a sounding board and not reciprocating, resenting her father for only caring about her when she succeeded at school, and wishing she had never been born so her mother would not be so unhappy. Eventually, she became convinced that she was not very nice, not very smart, and just plain weird compared to other girls her age. After failing a physics examination, she made a serious suicide attempt. Fortunately, Amanda survived and was successfully treated for her depression.

Amanda's relationship with her mother illustrates the role reversal and lack of boundaries that can characterize relationships between depressed adults and their children. By "boundaries," we mean a sense of separateness of one person's thoughts and feelings from those of the other person in the relationship. Using the child as a sounding board for personal problems, assuming that the child's opinions are one's own, or speaking for the child are all signs of this type of relationship. Younger children often go along with this sort of relationship because of a desire to please the parent, but in adolescence that desire conflicts with their increasing need for autonomy and personal identity.

If having such a relationship with a depressed parent had been her only problem, though, Amanda's development might have been less difficult. Her anxiety, her lack of social supports, and her lack of a more supportive parental relationship were all contributing factors. Her father, though apparently proud of her, showed interest in her mainly because of her achievements and what they represented in relation to his own unfulfilled dreams. He had little interest in his daughter as a person. Given the lack of supportive relationships in her life, Amanda became overly dependent on achievements. Therefore, the modest stress of failing an examination appeared, to her, to be insurmountable.

All of these factors speak to the need to support families of depressed individuals of all ages. When one member is debilitated by depression, the other members have to not only care for that person, but also meet each other's needs. They may not understand this, or may not be able to do this without outside help. Getting outside help may be essential to help the depressed parent manage his or her illness and feel better, and also to decrease the risk of mood disorders in the next generation. Let's look at some common issues in families struggling with depression.

Depression and Parenting

When parents are depressed, several things can happen, depending on the child's age and temperament. In infancy, children tend to have difficulty becoming securely "attached" (the state of feeling reassured by your parent's presence, and feeling special to your parent). This probably occurs because depression makes it hard for parents to respond in a consistently reassuring way when their baby is distressed. Fatigue, depressive withdrawal from others, and preoccupation with one's own inner life all contribute. Babies also use soothing experiences in the attachment relationship to learn how to soothe themselves, so infants with depressed parents often encounter difficulty in this area. For example, they may develop maladaptive behaviors such as crying a lot or, conversely, appearing passive and unresponsive to adult attention.

In the toddler years and beyond, children typically respond to a depressed parent with either care-giving or controlling behaviors. Care-giving behaviors imply a role reversal, where the child starts to parent the parent (at least emotionally). Care-giving children may take on more responsibility than is appropriate for their age, be overly conscientious, or appear overly agreeable in an attempt to protect the parent from emotional upset. In extreme cases, they become emotional sounding boards for the depressed parent, and psychological boundaries between depressed parent and child begin to blur. This means that the child has difficulty distinguishing his own wants and needs from his parent's.

Controlling behaviors may look like defiance, but their goal is different. Here, to reduce anxiety, the child tries to create a predictable environment when his parent is emotionally unpredictable. The child may appear bossy and demanding, telling his parent how to behave. For example, he may say to his parent, "Make sure I have a snack when I get home from school." The child may make certain rules and expect other family members to follow them. The depressed parent may accept these rules, to a degree, but consider the child willful and disobedient once he or she recovers from depression. A professional seeing only a "snapshot" of the family at this point in time might diagnose the child as having Oppositional Defiant Disorder (see page 30, Chapter 3). Incidentally, the parent in this case still needs to manage the child's difficult behavior (as discussed in Chapter 10), but with an understanding of how the behavior developed.

Each style—whether it is care-giving or controlling—creates additional problems in adolescence. The care-giving child may start to realize that he has missed out on childhood fun, and may try to catch up on it inappropriately. The psychological closeness with the depressed parent makes it difficult to develop autonomy, especially if boundaries have become blurred. Developing your identity is very complicated if your cannot distinguish your own desires from a parent's. The resulting confusion may put the teen at additional risk for depression himself. If the parent is still depressed when the child reaches adolescence, autonomy may also be associated with a great deal of guilt. Even the parent who has recovered may yearn for her compliant "model child," making it difficult to develop a healthy distance from the adolescent, and, in turn, making it difficult for the adolescent to experience autonomy.

A child who has been controlling may become more defiant in adolescence, feeling that the previously unpredictable parent has no right to tell him what to do. Controlling children often feel they "raised themselves," resulting in little respect for parents. It is tempting to assume they can fend for themselves, but behind the bravado they are just as vulnerable as their care-giving counterparts. These teens need considerable guidance from parents if they are to develop healthy relationships as adults.

Modeling a parent's depressive cognitive distortions also takes its toll on children over time. Pessimists raise pessimists, and children of depressed parents have a five-fold increased risk of depression compared to average adolescents (some of this may be genetic risk too, of course).

If there is one silver lining to the cloud, it's that "it takes one to know one." Nobody understands the experience of depression like someone who has lived it. Parents who have been depressed themselves and who accept that part of their lives are often more empathically attuned to their depressed children than anyone else. They can also become passionate advocates for their children, determined that their children are treated better than they were.

Talking about Depression

In situations where one or more family members is or has been depressed, open discussion of the illness is important. It is important that the depression not be a secret and that it be labeled and discussed so family members can become knowledgeable about what it is and how each can help. Without this kind of discussion, certain behaviors can be misunderstood, undermining family relationships. For example, children of depressed, withdrawn parents may assume incorrectly that the parent doesn't care for them anymore. Similarly, if a hospitalization is not explained, the children may feel abandoned. Siblings of a depressed child who cannot engage in his usual activities may notice the extra attention this behavior appears to elicit from parents. In response, they may copy depressive behaviors to gain attention for themselves. Once told that the depressed child has an illness, they are more likely to try to help him recover, rather than imitating his symptoms.

There are many reasons parents may hesitate to call depression by its proper name, including fear of social stigma, difficulty discussing emotional matters, embarrassment, and fear of overwhelming the child. In most cases, though, children are relieved when they know the truth. Having a label allows them to ask questions and inform themselves. It also explains why the depressed family member(s) sometimes are more upset or less responsive than a particular situation warrants, so children are less likely to blame themselves or feel rejected. For younger children, it reduces possible fears of "catching" the problem. Older children may be able to help out at home until the depressed family member recovers, but with a clear understanding that this is temporary and is going "above and beyond" what a child would normally be expected to do. Making this clear reduces the risk of role reversal becoming a more permanent aspect of the parent-child relationship.

As part of their discussions about depression, many families also discuss with whom to share the information. This reduces the risk of people outside the family stigmatizing the depressed individual. The booklet "Can I Catch It Like a Cold?" (see Bibliography) provides more ideas about discussing parental depression with children. Additionally, *Parenting Well When You're Depressed* is a comprehensive resource for maintaining a healthy family.

What Should a Parent Who Is Depressed Do?

- *Talk about the illness and its effect on your family.* Just having a name for the problem can be very helpful to some families.
- *Pay extra attention to adolescent emotional development* and your teenager's need for stronger connections to peers and increasing autonomy from your family.
- *Don't assume that because your child says nothing, he doesn't have concerns.*
- *Help children learn self-soothing strategies when upset (especially if your child was young when his parent was depressed), and model non-depressed ways of coping.* Relaxation techniques, writing down your feelings, taking a bath, going for a walk,

listening to (or playing) a favorite piece of music, spending time with a pet, or working on a favorite hobby or artistic pursuit can all be helpful in soothing yourself.

- *Take care of yourself.* Avoiding relapse is the most therapeutic thing you can do for your family. Involve yourself in activities, as recommended for your teen in Chapter 7, and maintain mental health follow-up if necessary.
- *Be honest with your family about how you feel, but emphasize what you are doing to overcome depression.* This will reduce the chances that your children will worry about you.
- *Resist the temptation to use a child or teen as a confidante.* Youngsters have enough to do dealing with their own problems; they don't need to be burdened with yours.
- *Talk to your spouse or a trusted friend.* He or she may be able to better handle some aspects of childrearing while you are depressed. Setting appropriate limits with children, for example, can be very difficult when you are depressed. Don't be afraid to modify "traditional" roles, if needed.
- *Focus on recovering from depression and gradually resume your usual responsibilities as you are able to.* Just like academic expectations have to be modified for depressed teens, your expectations of yourself in the work and family environments may have to be modified as well.
- *Ask for help outside the immediate family, if needed.* Sometimes it can feel as if having a depressed child can add to your own depression or make you feel responsible and guilty. Talk about these feelings with someone you can trust so they don't become burdensome and overwhelming.
- *Be prepared for times of crisis.* Create action plans with your family about how to handle "down" times or hospitalizations.

What Can the Non-Depressed Parent Do?

Having a depressed spouse, and perhaps a depressed teen as well, can be a tremendous burden on the "healthy" parent. Supporting the family may have to take precedence over career and other priorities for the time being, if everyone is to get through their depression without long-term problems. Beyond supporting your spouse and children as described above, consider obtaining some extra support for yourself. Even if it's just the occasional conversation with a good friend or individual or family counseling, it can make a dramatic difference at such a trying time. If you are religious, members of your faith community may also be supportive. As your spouse's depression begins to lift, resuming family activities may be both therapeutic for the depressed family member(s), and a source of hope and recreation for yourself.

Occasionally, you may also be in a position to recognize and address unhealthy interaction patterns occurring around the depressed individual(s) in your family. Returning to the example of Amanda, let's look at a L.E.A.P. plan her father could develop at the time when both Amanda and her mother were depressed.

Label thoughts and feelings: I'm getting really *frustrated* with Amanda. She used to do so well in school, but now she seems to be just average. How does she expect to make anything of herself at this rate? To be honest, I also *miss being proud* of her and being able to brag a bit to the neighbors about her. I'm *irritated* with my wife too. She doesn't seem to realize how important an education is. All she wants is for our daughter to sit around and listen to her complaints

Empathize with your teen: What the neighbors think isn't that important. It's Amanda's happiness and her future that matter. I wonder if Amanda is getting discouraged. After all, high school is harder than elementary school. Those constant talks with her mother may be draining her energy as well. Both of them seem rather unhappy.

Explore ways to respond: I wonder if Amanda could use some time away from her mother. She needs something enjoyable to focus on. Maybe I could get her back into the choir she used to enjoy. Maybe she'd like to go skating with me on the weekends, or play some tennis in the summer. If her schoolwork is too hard, maybe a tutor for the subjects she's finding difficult would help. Her teacher might also be able to tell me more about what she should be doing in this grade. If she still struggles and looks unhappy, maybe I should arrange a check-up with the doctor. My wife's problems go way back, and I don't understand them completely. She should probably see a therapist, if I could just get her to go! On the other hand, maybe she'll be more agreeable to seeing someone if Amanda is occupied with other things after school and stops listening to her so much. Alternatively, maybe if I offered to see someone with her, she would agree.

Apply alternative ideas/plan: I'll talk to Amanda's teachers and get her the best academic support I can. Then, I'll insist on at least one nonacademic after-school activity, and offer to take her out skating on weekends. I'll ask the doctor if she can recommend a therapist who could see my wife, or see my wife and me together

Pick a follow up time and plan ahead: I'll stay in touch with the teacher regularly, and keep my eyes open at home. If Amanda is still unhappy and struggling at school in a month, I'll have her see the doctor as well. I'll see if the therapist has any other suggestions.

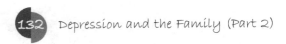

Exercise: Parenting Despite Depression

If you are currently depressed, pick one or more of the ideas from this chapter to develop a L.E.A.P. plan response to help yourself and work on it this week. If you are living with a spouse who is depressed, do a L.E.A.P. plan to either help yourself or help your spouse. Depending on your situation, you may wish to develop a L.E.A.P. plan to help your depressed spouse seek help. You may wish to develop a L.E.A.P. plan to help your family talk about depression and its impact on family members. Use your good judgment to decide who to involve in your L.E.A.P. plan and how.

Key Points

If you are not yourself affected by depression, review the exercise from the previous chapter on page 122.

What should parents do when one or both is depressed?
- Talk about the illness and its effect on the family.
- Pay extra attention to children's emotional development.
- Help children learn self-soothing (especially if the child was young when his parent was depressed).
- Take care of yourself. Avoiding relapse is the most therapeutic thing you can do for your family.
- Don't burden children with your troubles.
- Involve your spouse in parenting.
- Ask for outside help if needed.

Your L.E.A.P. plan response for this week is:

The situation: _____

_____

_____

_____

_____

Label your thoughts and feelings: _____

_____

_____

_____

_____

Empathize with your teen: _____

_____

_____

_____

_____

Explore ways to respond: _____

_____

_____

_____

_____

Apply alternative idea/plan: _____

_____

_____

_____

_____

Pick a follow-up time and plan ahead: _____

_____

_____

_____

_____

Suicidal Behavior
and Other Crises

Today, we'll talk about one of the most feared aspects of depression in children and teens: crisis situations. These are situations that involve physical danger to the child or those around the child. Parents find themselves overwhelmed, and respond by calling 911, going to the emergency department, or sometimes involving Children's Aid. To deal with a crisis effectively, parents must:

- contain their own feelings about what's happening,
- do what is in the child's best interest quickly, and
- then work on a long-term plan, usually with the aid of a professional.

Parents are often frustrated when they arrive at the emergency department hoping for a "solution" to the teen's extreme behavior and are told only that their child does or does not need to be hospitalized. Nevertheless, this is usually what happens, and with good reason. In the short-term, the only solution is to ensure that the behavior does not repeat itself (i.e., that everyone is safe). Hospitalization or close monitoring at home (depending on the level of risk) is what's

Progress Check

Any success with the family-related L.E.A.P. plan(s)? Be patient, if not. Family interactions are among the hardest patterns to change. Keep trying!

needed. In the long-term, further treatment for your teen and family are needed to deal with the causes of the behavior (for example, addressing depression in the suicidal teen), but this will not occur in the emergency room. Consistent follow-up with a mental health professional or a team of professionals over several months (at minimum) will address the longer-term issues.

Suicidal Threats

Threats of suicide or attempts at suicide are usually the most difficult crises for families of depressed children. It's important to remember, however, that although thoughts of self-harm are almost universal among depressed children, attempts are far fewer. About 20 to 25 percent of teens with major depression attempt suicide at some point before age 20. Children or teens who actually die by suicide are rare (less than 4 percent of teens with major depression, most of these in the late teens). These figures are still much higher than in the general population, though, so threats of suicide must be taken seriously. Depressed girls are more likely to attempt suicide, but depressed boys more often complete suicide (they often use more lethal methods).

Some books have long lists of "signs" to look for in assessing children's suicidality. Unfortunately, these create the false impression that you can evaluate this risk yourself. This is simply not true. Even experienced professionals have difficulty predicting who will attempt suicide and who will not, and even the correct predictions are rarely accurate for more than the next 24 to 48 hours. Trust your instincts. Go to the nearest hospital emergency department if you believe your child is at risk. Be extra suspicious if:

1. *Your child has a friend who talks about suicide or has recently engaged in suicidal behavior* (in this case, there is potential for a suicide "pact" among peers);
2. *Your child starts to give away her possessions*; or
3. *There has been a recent loss of a close relationship or a source of pride* (for example, losing a major competition or failing an examination).

Conversely, if your child has a habit of threatening "I'll kill myself if you don't give me what I want," recognize this for what it is: an expression of anger. On its own, this means little. If there are other recent changes in your child's behavior, however, it may be worth checking with a professional.

Also, beware of the impulsive child who takes a handful of pills in front of you to "make a statement." Depending on the pills, they could result in an inadvertent fatality (for example, Tylenol can destroy the liver). Following up with an emergency visit is often a good idea. The experience of being made to swallow charcoal (to neutralize stomach contents) or having a tube inserted down the throat can also be noxious enough to deter children and teens from repeating this behavior.

Dealing with Suicidal Risk

Good rules of thumb for dealing with suicidal risk include:

- *If you think your child is at risk, go to the nearest emergency department.*
- If your child is sent home from the emergency room, remember that *you can return there if the situation deteriorates* before your next scheduled visit with the doctor.
- It doesn't hurt to **lock up medications, sharp objects, or weapons** if your child is or has recently been suicidal.
- *Safety concerns always take priority over privacy concerns* (i.e., this is the one situation where it's OK to search your teen's room).
- *Children or teens with suicidal tendencies usually stabilize more readily if they learn to trust one therapist or one group of professionals.* This is not the time to "shop around" for new treatments or additional assessments if you and your teen are already working with competent professionals. (Trust takes time to develop, so don't necessarily leave it to your teen's judgment as to whether or not a therapist is competent.)
- *Hospitalization can provide a temporary safe haven for the suicidal child or teen, but it doesn't really solve the problem.* If prolonged, it can result in your child becoming overly dependent on staff (a detrimental result). Most hospitals these days insist on family involvement from the start, and begin planning for the child's return home starting on the day of arrival.
- Teens who are uncooperative with hospitalization (for example, they refuse to go into the hospital or threaten to run away from it) *may have to be admitted to the hospital on an involuntary basis.* In Canada, this may require transfer to a so-called "Schedule 1" facility, which is equipped to prevent patients from leaving. They do have a right to legal advice, however, and can challenge their involuntary status. In most states in the U.S., parents can have children who are not of legal age admitted to the hospital without their consent. Check with your child's doctor if considering this option.

As children and teens recover from their crises, it is also important to allow for a gradual increase in freedoms and responsibilities. Teens who are struggling with autonomy can find a "hovering" parent very difficult to live with, sometimes exacerbating their mood. The same principles apply as in a younger child: when the teen behaves responsibly, demonstrating the ability to handle more independence, greater freedom is granted, a little bit at a time.

Finally, let us cite the old adage "an ounce of prevention is worth a pound of cure." If you see your child or teen deteriorating, call the doctor or mental health professional who usually sees her. Scheduling an earlier appointment with a familiar mental health professional is often far more helpful than ending up with an unfamiliar professional in the emergency department.

Why Do Some Teens Repeatedly Harm Themselves?

A variation on suicidal behavior (sometimes termed "parasuicidal behavior" or "suicidal gestures") occurs in teens who harm themselves repeatedly in ways unlikely to cause death. Common examples include superficial cutting of the forearms or other areas of the body, self-inflicted cigarette burns, hitting oneself with a fist or an object, or hitting one's head against a wall or hard object. It used to be thought that these displays represented part of an emerging personality disorder, but recent studies have shown that this is not always the case. Other reasons for such behavior can include:

- The teen has feelings of guilt or worthlessness that are part of depression.
- The teen is trying to regulate unpleasant feelings (see below).
- The teen is expressing anger or desire for someone's attention (for example, from a parent or a boyfriend).

Some teens engage in these behaviors only in the midst of a depressive episode, as in the example below.

Brian: *Brian was deeply depressed, but determined to continue attending school. He was suspended after repeatedly gouging his face with scissors. The teachers felt they could not monitor him closely enough to ensure his safety, and other students were very disturbed by witnessing his self-mutilation. Interestingly, Brian engaged in no self-harm at all after his mood improved with antidepressant medication. He went back to his fellow students and explained the nature of depression and how it affected him in a class presentation. He explained his previous self-harm behavior by saying, "At the time, I felt I deserved to be punished. I felt less guilty after I punished myself." The following year, he graduated as class valedictorian.*

For other teens, self-harm behavior represents a way of regulating unpleasant feelings. When the body is physically injured, endorphins are released. These are brain chemicals that are natural pain-killers, but they also have a mood-elevating effect. Thus, by inflicting physical pain on themselves, these teens numb their emotional pain. Some claim to eventually not feel the physical pain at all. For these teens, self-harm behavior can be decreased by helping them use alternative mood regulation strategies, such as those described earlier in Chapters 7, 8, and 9. Incidentally, regular physical exercise releases endorphins too, so encouraging a sports activity can also be helpful.

Finally, some teens harm themselves to demonstrate anger or gain attention. This is especially likely in those who engage in self-harm in front of other people (usually family, most often during or after an argument). These teens often benefit from all of the strategies discussed in the chapter on anger. They usually need more consistent limits and a parent who can remain calm and not be drawn into arguments. It is important not to allow threats of self-harm to change your parenting decisions. This would simply reinforce your teen's negative behaviors. Instead, you should come up with a L.E.A.P. plan in relation to anger, as Marcy's parents did in Chapter 10. The exception would be if your teen was threatening serious self-harm in front of you (for example, brandishing a knife or firearm), in which case a call to emergency services would be indicated.

Example: Brian's Cutting

Although Brian ultimately had a very positive outcome, the road there was not an easy one for his family. His mother received a call at work one day, indicating he had been sent to the emergency room by ambulance after the teacher found his face covered in blood from a cutting incident in the school washroom. It's difficult to think in terms of a L.E.A.P. plan under such duress, but Brian's mother's reaction did follow the same basic steps:

Label thoughts and feelings: Oh, God. What has he done to himself? I'm *worried sick* he's done something permanent this time. Why wouldn't they tell me the details? Did he lose an eye? Is his life in danger? Why won't anyone tell me? And even if he's OK, with something like this, the school will never take him back. His education is ruined! And who would hire someone with a disfigured face?

Empathize with your teen: This panic isn't going to help Brian. I have to take a few deep breaths and calm down, for his sake. He's probably even more scared of what's happening to him. I have to be strong and hopeful to keep him going.

Explore ways to respond: Maybe I can talk to the doctor first, before I see Brian. Then, I can offer him some realistic reassurance based on what I learn. I'll find out what they're planning to do as well. If he's staying at the hospital a while, I'll get my husband to look after his sister after school so I can stay with Brian. I should take it one step at a time. Worrying about the future right now won't help.

Apply alternative ideas/plan: I'm at the hospital now. I'll ask the nurse who Brian's doctor is, and find a phone to contact my husband.

Pick a follow up time and plan ahead: Here goes. If we get through the next 24 hours, we can relax a bit and plan what to do longer term.

Exercise: A Plan for Crisis Situations

Have you dealt with suicidal behavior or other crises with your depressed child or teen? Would you do anything differently if a similar situation happened now? Take a moment to do a L.E.A.P. plan for a crisis, recognizing that (unless your child or teen is currently in a crisis) you will file this one for future reference. Pick a situation that seems possible (even if you hope it never happens), and that you have not previously figured out how to handle. Also choose a L.E.A.P. plan response from a previous chapter to practice this week.

The Worst-Case Scenario

Occasionally, a teen does end his or her life despite our best efforts. It is a devastating event to those left behind, and feelings about it are difficult to resolve. We include the following example only for those who have encountered such a tragedy, or the related tragedy of a teen who is permanently debilitated by a serious suicide attempt.

Lowell: *Lowell had been hospitalized for depression in his final year of high school. His family was very concerned that he return to school to get his diploma. Lowell's older brother had been accepted to law school, and Lowell was expected to aspire to a profession as well. Lowell, on the other hand, liked to tinker with cars and machinery, but struggled academically. Always a social loner, he confided in his mother one day that he would like to go to a technical school to become a mechanic rather than attending the college preparatory program at the local high school. His mother sympathized, but his father felt this would be "selling himself short" so he went to the prep program. The only one in the family Lowell felt close to was his brother. They went to baseball games together, and had a similar sense of humor. When Lowell's brother moved away to go to law school, Lowell became profoundly depressed, lost weight, couldn't sleep, became convinced that he was "marked" by the devil and receiving messages from him via the television, and made an unsuccessful attempt to hang himself.*

While hospitalized, Lowell made slow but steady progress with antidepressant medication. He didn't respond very well to the first medication, but seemed to do better on the second one. He liked the nurses, and they liked him. Unlike some of the other patients, he was polite, soft-spoken, and young enough to turn his life around (or so they thought). Besides the occasional talk with his brother, this was the only situation where Lowell had felt truly understood. He liked his doctor, too. She patiently went over his symptoms and side effects every day and plotted them on a chart to see if he needed more medication, less medication, or something else that might be helpful.

After four months, he was considered ready for discharge and began getting passes to go outside the hospital with his family. Since the family lived at some distance from the hospital, the plan was to have Lowell's family doctor follow up on the medication. Eventually, a date was set for discharge. The next day was Friday, and Lowell was given his first weekend pass outside the hospital (he had gone out on several uneventful day passes with family members at this point).

Friday morning, one of the nurses commented that Lowell seemed out of sorts, but she couldn't describe exactly what was wrong. Lowell's doctor talked to him, reviewing all his symptoms again, including any thoughts of suicide, but his answers were no different from the day before. Then she asked about the weekend, and he said he was planning to go to a baseball game with his brother who was visiting. Was anything bothering him or making him upset? He replied, "No," but seemed fidgety. The doctor remarked on the minor movements. "Just want to get going, get out in the sunshine," he said. "You're sure that's all it is?" she asked. "Positive," he replied.

The doctor noted the discussion, and went on to the next patient. After lunch, Lowell put his things together and took a telephone call. "It's my brother," he said. "He's waiting in the lobby." Lowell had never lied before, so everyone accepted this. Lowell got on the elevator with his things. A half hour later, the doctor was called to the telephone. It was another doctor in the emergency department of the hospital down the street. "I have some unfortunate news. A subway jumper was brought to our emergency department," he said. "He had a vial of antidepressants in his pocket with your name on them." She asked his condition. "Dead on arrival" was the reply.

Lowell died over fifteen years ago, when I (KM) was a trainee in psychiatry, yet I've reviewed the events of that last Friday of his life a thousand times or more. What did we miss? What did the nurse pick up on that I didn't detect? Was it the fact that he was only a few years younger than I was that clouded my judgment? Why didn't I insist his brother meet him on the ward instead of letting him go down the elevator alone? There will never be answers to those questions. All we can do is try to learn from these events some of the factors that might have signaled trouble for Lowell.

Factors that might have suggested a high risk of suicide for Lowell include:
- being male (girls make more attempts, but boys are more likely to kill themselves);
- having made a previous attempt;
- using highly lethal methods (hanging, subway or bridge jumps, and using a firearm are among the most lethal);
- lack of social supports;
- having psychotic features (the ideas about the devil messages from the television); and
- loss of a close relationship (his brother away at law school).

Lowell was anticipating further losses that day, having been informed that he was about to be discharged. He would lose the doctors and nurses who had cared for him, and the familiar hospital environment.

One thing that did not place him at risk was the inquiry about suicidal symptoms. We know that asking about suicide does not prompt it. In fact, when parents and professionals open the subject for discussion, this is sometimes a relief to teens burdened by suicidal thoughts. If you suspect your teen may be having such thoughts, ask.

Finally, all of us affected by such tragedies must learn to accept that no matter how diligent and thoughtful we may be, we cannot always save people from themselves. There are always regrets in such situations: What if I had done this? What if I had noticed that? Hopefully, those regrets result in better choices for the future. Lowell's case was the subject of an inquiry, and changes to hospital procedures concerning passes and trainee supervision occurred as a result of this type of careful examination. Ultimately, though, Lowell chose to end his life. Perhaps it could have been prevented at that particular time. If it had been, however, there would still have come a time when Lowell would again be given the liberty to make that choice. We cannot hospitalize people indefinitely to ensure absolute safety. It simply wouldn't be fair to them. As concerned doctors and parents, we can help suicidal teens, but we can't make them want to live.

Key Points

- If you think your child is at risk of harming herself, go to the nearest emergency department.
- If your child is sent home from the emergency room, remember that you can return there if the situation deteriorates before your next scheduled visit with the doctor.
- It doesn't hurt to lock up medications, sharp objects, or weapons if your child is or has recently been suicidal.
- Safety concerns always take priority over privacy concerns (i.e., this is the one situation where it's OK to search your child's room).
- Children with suicidal tendencies usually stabilize more readily if they learn to trust one therapist or one group of professionals. This is not the time to "shop around" for new treatments or additional assessments.
- Repeated self-harm behavior may decrease when depression is treated, alternative ways are found to regulate feelings, and/or teens experience clear, consistent limits and parents who are not manipulated by threats.
- Talking about suicide doesn't cause it. If you suspect your child or teen may be having suicidal thoughts, don't be afraid to ask.

Your L.E.A.P. plan response for this week is:

The hypothetical situation: _____

_____

_____

_____

_____

Label your thoughts and feelings: _____

_____

_____

_____

_____

Empathize with your teen: _____

_____

_____

_____

_____

Explore ways to respond: _____

_____

_____

_____

_____

Apply alternative ideas/plan: _____

_____

_____

_____

_____

Pick a follow-up time and plan ahead: _____

_____

_____

_____

15

Medications and Depression

Depression has been linked to changes in the levels of neurotransmitters (messenger chemicals that help brain cells communicate). Noradrenaline (also known as norepinephrine) and serotonin are the two neurotransmitters most consistently linked to depression. It is believed that most people with major depression have lower than average levels of one or both of these chemicals in certain parts of the brain. In some depressed people, particularly those with milder forms of depression, neurotransmitter levels may not be unusual. Their depressed feelings likely come from difficulty handling the life circumstances they are facing. Just because someone's circumstances are difficult, however, does not mean that there cannot also be a biochemical reason for their depression.

Medications address the biochemical part of depression by increasing depressed people's levels of noradrenaline or serotonin, boosting them back into the average range. Some antidepressant medications act mainly on noradrenaline, some act mainly on serotonin, and some act on both.

This chapter reviews the medications that are most often prescribed for teens with depression and discusses the parents' role in making decisions and/or supporting medication treatment.

Progress Check

Here's the weekly reminder: Follow-up on those L.E.A.P. plans!

Deciding Whether Medications Are Right for Your Teen

In every case, the potential risks and benefits of a medication should be discussed with your child's doctor before starting. Every medication has potential side effects (*potential* because not everyone gets them), but in a seriously depressed youngster these are usually worth tolerating in order to obtain relief from the symptoms of depression.

In a mildly or moderately depressed youngster, medication may not be necessary, especially if effective psychotherapy (treatment that involves talking to a mental health provider on a regular basis) is available. For depression, several forms of psychotherapy have been shown to be effective in adults:

1. CBT, described in Chapter 9, and

2. Interpersonal Therapy (IPT)—This form of therapy focuses less on the role of depressive thinking in depression than CBT does, and more on the role of interpersonal relationships. Grief, changes in one's roles and responsibilities (for example, starting high school, teen-parent disagreements or other conflicts with others about roles and responsibilities), and lack of interpersonal skills can all cause problems that may contribute to depression. IPT helps people address one or more of these problems by focusing on them systematically in a series of sessions with a therapist.

Positive results have been reported for both of these therapies in children and teens as well (but there have been fewer studies to date than with adults).

Rather than turning away from medication too quickly, however, consider the risks of *not* providing medication. Psychotherapy takes time to become effective (somewhat longer than medication, in most cases), and a moderately depressed child can deteriorate quickly. Allowing impairment at school and with peers to persist can also have devastating consequences for some teens. On the other hand, relapse risk is somewhat lower with CBT than with medication. That is, depressed people who are effectively treated with CBT alone are less likely to experience depression again than those who are treated with medication alone. If available, consider combining psychological and medical treatments to give your child the best chance of good functioning now and in the future. If your teen continues to use coping strategies learned in CBT, it may be possible to safely taper the medication within a year or so.

Types of Medication

Older antidepressants (so-called "tricyclics") targeted both serotonin and noradrenaline, but also affected other neurotransmitters, unrelated to depression. The most troublesome effects were on the neurotransmitter acetylcholine, resulting in so-called "anticholinergic" side effects (acetylcholine was reduced). These effects included dry mouth, constipation, sedation, and (less commonly) flushing, blurred vision, or urinary retention. In children, there were also several reports of irregular heartbeat with these medications. Therefore, they are currently only used if other medications fail, and always with monitoring of your child's electrocardiogram (a test that monitors the electrical activity of the heart).

Newer medications called "SSRIs" (selective serotonin reuptake inhibitors) do not have these problems, and there is some evidence that they are more effective in teens than the older tricyclics. SSRIs increase only the brain chemical serotonin, and are so-called because they prevent the "reuptake" (removal and breakdown) of this brain chemical. They all work in 70 to 80 percent of depressed children and teens (no one drug stands out), but it is impossible to predict which child will respond to which medication, so some children must try more than one. If another member of the immediate family has done well with a particular drug, however, it is usually worth trying this one in the affected child.

Effective doses in children are highly variable, so most doctors start at a low dose and increase it every couple of weeks as long as the child does not have significant side effects. All these medications take from two to eight weeks to become fully effective *after the last dosage increase*. Effectiveness usually is evident from improvements in eating and sleeping patterns (early changes), with improvements in mood becoming evident later. Increasing the dose every couple of weeks may result in "overshooting" the optimum dose a bit, given that full benefits may not occur until eight weeks after the last increase. On the other hand, waiting eight weeks between dosage changes would prolong the process unreasonably, so two-week intervals are generally considered good practice. In the hospital (where there is additional monitoring), dosage can be increased more quickly.

Side Effects

Like all medications, SSRIs can have potential side effects. Common ones include:

- *Nausea or upset stomach,* especially during the first week or so after starting medication or after a dosage increase.
- *Sedation (tiredness or sleepiness) or activation (having more energy) can also occur with these medications.* Of the five currently prescribed, fluvoxamine (Luvox) is more often sedating, fluoxetine (Prozac) and paroxetine (Paxil) are more often activating, and sertraline (Zoloft) and citalopram (Celexa) are in between. We use the term "more often" because children and teens vary greatly in their responses, and the same medication may sedate one child and activate another. By having either morning (for activating medication) or evening (for sedating medication) dosing, these problems can often be avoided. Youngsters appear to be somewhat more sensitive to the activating effects of SSRIs than adults are, so the more sedating and "in between" medications have increased in popularity with children recently.

- *Headaches* are less common side effects, but can occur in children who are predisposed.
- *Loss of sexual interest can occur.*
- *Flu-like symptoms can occur if they are stopped suddenly* (except for Prozac, which leaves the body very gradually). Note, however, that none of these medications are addictive, in the sense that they do not induce a "high," and the body does not develop a need for ever-increasing doses over time (termed "tolerance"). Dosage adjustments are made according to your child's response to the medication, and sometimes in response to physical growth. Teens who grow quickly or gain substantial weight quickly may need more medication.
- *Weight change can occur.* Weight gain is more common than weight loss, but some of these medications (for example, Prozac) can also curb appetite in some people. With good eating habits, medication-related weight change is usually not great. Remember, though, that appetite changes often accompany depression and remit as depression improves. Thus, a teen whose appetite has been suppressed by depression for several months may appear to gain substantial weight when the depression is medically treated.

Overall, SSRIs are remarkably well tolerated compared to other psychiatric medications. The one exception occurs in people predisposed to bipolar disorder, a condition where elated or irritable mood episodes occur alternating with depressive ones. In these people, SSRIs (or any other antidepressant medications) can sometimes trigger manic episodes. People with close relatives who have bipolar disorder may also be at risk for this reaction.

How Long Should Teens Remain on Medication?

Once your child is on the right dose and some benefit is observed, it is usually worth continuing the medication for at least six months to one year. There is some evidence that a year may be preferable, to reduce the risk of relapse if your child is still in a depressive episode at six months. Then, an attempt to taper the medication (decreasing the dose very gradually) can be made, especially if your child has developed coping skills from a cognitive-behavioral psychotherapy program. The goal is to have your child on the minimum dose needed. In some children, the medication can be discontinued at this point, while others require medication longer term. Tapering is usually best done at a time of average life stress, to minimize the risk of relapse. If your child grows or encounters a greater-than-average degree of life stress, a dosage increase may be needed.

Long-term effects of SSRIs in children and teens are not well studied. These medications have not yet been used in children long enough for such studies to have been done. Adults sometimes develop an apathetic state termed "amotivational syndrome"

Do SSRIs Increase Suicide Risk?

Recently, concerns have been raised about increased suicidal ideation in children and teens taking certain antidepressants. (Suicidal ideation means that when interviewed, these teens reported often thinking about suicide.) As a result, the FDA has cautioned physicians about prescribing most of the newer antidepressants to children and has encouraged careful monitoring of all patients on these medications. If your child or teen is taking one of these medications and obtaining benefit, however, talk to the doctor before stopping it. Abruptly stopping medication can leave your child vulnerable to a relapse of depression, which can also be harmful. Talk to the doctor about all the options before deciding how to proceed.

While studies to date show that the rate of suicidal ideation is somewhat higher in depressed children on these medications than in those taking a placebo (sugar pill), that does not mean that the medications necessarily cause suicidal ideation. In fact, the majority of children on these medications experienced no suicidal ideation. More studies are needed to determine the reason why *some* children who take these medications develop suicidal thoughts. In the meantime, it's probably best to do a careful analysis of risks and benefits with the doctor if you are thinking of having your child try antidepressants, and especially if your child is already taking one of these medications.

and there are case reports of this syndrome in adolescents, but it tends to resolve with dosage reduction. Several children and teens at our centre have required SSRIs for more than a couple of years, and "so far so good." They seem to grow and develop normally. There is even some animal evidence that SSRIs may increase the body's ability to produce serotonin in the brain, but this has not yet been studied in humans.

Newer Medications

The "third generation" of antidepressants (so-called because they are the newest, and were developed after the tricyclics and the SSRI's) include venlafaxine (Effexor), bupropion (Wellbutrin or Zyban), nefazedone (Serzone), and reboxitine (Remiron). These are usually reserved for children and teens who don't respond to SSRIs or cannot tolerate them. Bupropion targets mainly noradrenaline, while the others target noradrenaline and serotonin, but with fewer side effects than the old tricyclics. Experience with these medications in children and adolescents is limited.

Serzone was recently taken off the market in Canada because it was linked to liver damage in some people, and concerns about Effexor and suicidal ideation have been raised, as discussed above. Activation is sometimes a problem with bupropion. For bupropion, also note that it is used in smoking cessation under the name Zyban. It is important that people do not mix Zyban with other antidepressants unless this occurs under a doctor's supervision. Remiron is the newest of the group, and experience in young people is very limited. New antidepressants come on the market quickly, however, and some of the information in this paragraph may change within a year or two.

All antidepressants can be sedating in combination with other sedating drugs (such as certain antihistamines), so check with a doctor on these combinations. Another popular combination to avoid is antidepressant + alcohol (both sedating). If it's difficult to monitor this with your teen, at least stress the importance of having one drink only and someone sober to drive him home.

Why Does My Teen Object to Medication?

There are many reasons why teens feel uncomfortable with taking antidepressant medications. Some common ones include:

- **Side effects,** especially side effects that might result in embarrassment with others, are often feared by teens. If you notice them, don't be shy about asking the doctor (or encouraging your teen to ask the doctor) how these might be addressed. Sexual side effects, most commonly decreased sexual interest, can be particularly troubling for teens, and not always easy to treat. If they persist (and your teen actually mentions them to you), try emphasizing the time-limited nature of medication treatment and encourage regular discussions with the doctor about alternatives that may not have these side effects, as well as discussions about when the medication can be reduced.

- **Forgetting is a common complaint**, but can also be a cover for other concerns about medication. It is problematic with antidepressants, because they only work when a certain level of the drug is maintained in the bloodstream, and this does not occur when doses are missed. Try having your child take the medication at the same place at the same time every day, preferably with a meal in the kitchen where you can provide a discreet reminder if needed. If forgetting still occurs regularly, talk calmly about what your child considers the pros and cons of medication, to see if you can determine the real concern.

- **"Drugs are bad for you."** This one's tricky, because we all agree that it would be desirable to keep your teen off *illicit* drugs if possible. Try distinguishing between medicines that replace what the body is lacking (in this case, serotonin) and street drugs that do not support any bodily need but are merely taken for the pleasure of getting high. A medical analogy sometimes helps (e.g., diabetics need insulin, but that's not a drug; people who don't eat well sometimes need vitamins, but that's not a drug).

- **"I won't be myself on it."** Here, the teenager's concern about his emerging identity gets mixed up with concern about medication.

Try explaining, "It doesn't make you do things you *don't* want to do; it just makes it easier to do things you *do* want to do." Sometimes, the best thing to do is to contract for a time-limited trial (usually, a few weeks) and then agree to reevaluate things. If your teen actually tries the medication, chances are he will describe feeling either "just like my old self" or "like a better version of me," but not like a different person.

- *"My parents are trying to make me take medication, and I make my own decisions."* Here, the adolescent concern about developing independence from the family gets mixed up with concern about medication. Try emphasizing that your teen does have some choice in the matter, and that your power to control medication intake is limited. After all, most teens are too big to be restrained and force-fed their tablets. In fact, once they are of legal age, teens are entitled to make their own decisions about medical care. At the same time, encourage an informed decision based on considering the risks of *not* taking medication (for example, academic problems or debilitating anxiety that may actually limit independence) as well as the risks of taking it.

- *"I don't want anyone else to know I take it."* Fear of appearing weak or different may be behind this statement. Fortunately, in most cases people outside the family don't need to know. Most of these medications are taken once a day, either in the morning or evening, so they can easily be taken at home. Going to camp may be a bit problematic, but find out in advance who would be providing the medication and discuss with them (or have your teen discuss with them) the best way of doing this so that embarrassment is minimized.

- *"I like to drink at parties."* Alcohol is one of the most commonly used drugs, but it is still a drug and it does interact with antidepressants. Discuss ways of having fun that don't involve alcohol, perhaps try out some nonalcoholic beers or wines, and if there is no way to avoid a particular social event involving alcohol (a graduation party, for example) encourage very limited consumption (nursing one drink all evening) and no driving under any circumstances. Antidepressant/alcohol interaction results in sedation, making drinking and driving even more dangerous than otherwise. If your teen is young enough to go to chaperoned parties, you can also try enlisting the help of parents at the parties in making sure alcohol is not served.

Izzy: *Izzy, age sixteen, had been depressed and anxious for several months. He had the sweatiest palms I (KM) ever encountered when we first met; he stammered and could hardly sit still because he was so anxious. He became noticeably calmer after* *about four weeks of treatment with an antidepressant medication, and his mood brightened as well. He continued on the medication for some time, but after about five months on it he reported that it "stopped working" and it was causing him to feel more tired than usual, although he had never experienced this side effect before. I clarified that he was taking it in the evening, as prescribed, and not during the day when it could produce drowsiness. I asked how regularly he took it. "All the time, doc, all the time," he replied.*

Later in the appointment, his father joined us and presented me with a pill bottle that was still half full. I confronted Izzy with this fact. He explained: "It's summer, doc, and me and my friends like to party, you know? But you said not to mix this with drinks or pot, and you can't party without drinks or pot, you know. So I just don't take it when I party. Sometimes I take an extra one the next day, if I remember."

In the discussion that followed, I explained that taking an extra one probably induced his tiredness, and missed doses due to frequent partying were limiting the beneficial effects of his medication. I suggested resuming a more regular pattern of medication use, and asked in more detail about his alcohol and marijuana use. Use of both of these substances was more substantial than he had initially admitted, and I referred him to a colleague specializing in helping teens with substance abuse problems. We also negotiated for temporary parental supervision of Izzy's medication (that is, taking it in front of a parent each day), with the understanding that this would stop when he had shown he could manage his medication responsibly for at least a month. Recreational activities other than "partying" were also encouraged.

Alcohol is particularly tempting for teens who suffer from anxiety as well as depression. Because it is a mild sedative, they will sometimes use it "to calm the nerves," especially in social situations. They often find that their nerves are worse afterwards, however, as withdrawal from alcohol makes them edgy and interrupts their sleep. I often point out these disadvantages to teens when doing a comparison of alcohol versus antidepressant medication for treating nerves. Comparing the pros and cons is often more helpful than preaching abstinence, because it respects the teen's ability to make choices.

What about Natural Options?

Some people are averse to medications because they believe them to be "unnatural," as most have been manufactured in laboratories. They would prefer something derived from a plant or other natural substance. I usually advise evaluating the risks and benefits of both options. In terms of risks, the "naturals" are often touted as having fewer side effects, but it is also more difficult to determine their purity (important in deciding about dosage). There is often a great deal of variability from one brand to another, and the inactive ingredients (apart from the active substance itself) are often not spelled out. With a medication developed in a laboratory, you know more precisely what you are taking.

In terms of benefit, there are some individuals (including some in our practice) who have responded to herbal remedies and many who have responded to prescribed medication. One criterion for approval of prescribed medication, however, is that efficacy has been demonstrated above and beyond the efficacy of a placebo (sugar pill) in large numbers of people. Over-the-counter herbal remedies do not have to meet this standard.

The most commonly used herbal remedy for depression is St. John's Wort. Unlike many such remedies, St. John's Wort has been subjected to a number of studies in adults, both in Europe and North America. Results from Europe appeared very promising, but a large North American study recently could not demonstrate efficacy above and beyond the efficacy of a placebo. Still, if you or your teen is very concerned about the risk of side effects with pharmaceuticals and/or has failed to respond to one or more standard antidepressant medications, it may be worth considering. Studies tell you how hundreds of people respond *on the average*, but they cannot predict how a particular individual will respond. No studies to date have examined St. John's Wort in adolescents or children. St. John's Wort can interact with some prescription drugs, particularly other antidepressants, so check with your doctor or pharmacist first if your teen is already taking another medication.

Dealing with Different Opinions on Medication

Teens are not the only ones who sometimes have concerns about taking medication for depression. Adults in the teen's life can influence his attitude as well. Many parents who recognize the benefits of antidepressant medication for their teen struggle with the conflicting opinions of school personnel, grandparents, and even spouses. Interestingly, when dealing with these adults, a problem-solving approach that includes some empathy often works well. It reduces the tendency for people to argue or to blame each other, by keeping the focus on the problem, and empathic comments invariably increase the level of trust in the relationship. Thus, you can do a L.E.A.P. plan for these people, as well as for your teen.

In Izzy's case, for example, his mother was initially quite concerned about the risks of antidepressant medication. Her own mother had been hospitalized for psychiatric reasons many years ago, and she still remembered the horrible effects of insulin shock, large doses of antipsychotic drugs, and other pharmaceutical treatments of that era. Explanations of how much more specific, better studied, and less toxic current treatments are did little to reduce her fears. Fortunately, Izzy's father was able to discuss the situation with his wife. Here is his L.E.A.P. plan:

Label thoughts and feelings: I'm so *worried* about Izzy. He's thin, he's not doing any school work, he's in his room with his music all day, and he doesn't sleep. We've tried counseling, but he just can't get his life back on track. Medication might make the difference, but Helen (wife) refuses to consider it. It's so *frustrating!*

Empathize with your teen: Maybe if I'd gone through what Helen went through with her mom I'd be skeptical of medication too. Whenever I try to convince her the newer treatments are better, she just feels pressured to give in, and gets more scared for Izzy. She must be really scared of reliving the past.

Explore ways to respond: Maybe I can get her to agree to a little bit of medication for a short period of time, just to make sure that Izzy is OK on it. Then, if she sees that he doesn't have horrible side effects, she may be willing to consider giving him a therapeutic amount. I could invite her to join us at the doctor's too, so she can ask about what happened to her mother, as well as what might happen to Izzy. She could get her mother's records from the hospital, and the doctor could help her make sense of them and explain exactly how things are different now.

Apply alternative ideas/plan: I'll make these suggestions to Helen, and see if she'd consider even one of them. (Helen agreed to see the doctor and maybe try Izzy on a small amount of medication with close supervision by herself, but declined to pursue her mother's medical record.)

Pick a follow up time and plan ahead: After a week on the smallest amount of medication, I'll talk to Helen again to see if she'll agree to another step.

Exercise: Getting the Medication In

Is your child or teen on medication? What type of medication(s)? What has your experience been with medication(s) so far? What problems have you encountered? Is it difficult to address your concerns with the prescribing physician? How could this be handled? (You may be surprised to know that even professionals sometimes respond remarkably well to a thoughtful L.E.A.P. approach.)

Have you run into problems having the medication administered to your child or teen at school (if needed) or at camp? Are there other members of the family or extended family who question your teen's need for medication? How is this handled best?

Is your child insisting that others not know about the medication? Is this reasonable? Is it difficult to get your child or teen to take medication? What helps? Write down helpful ideas to try with your teen on the last page of this chapter.

If your teen is *not* on medication and you think it might help, discuss this option with him objectively, including possible advantages and disadvantages. Make it clear that you respect his opinion on the subject, but would like to explore it further with a professional. Then, see if he will go to the family doctor with you. Sometimes a check-up that addresses psychological as well as physical concerns is more acceptable to a teen initially than being sent to a "shrink." If your teen is agreeable, the family doctor can then prescribe antidepressant medication, or refer to a psychiatrist if this is preferred. If not, at least the doctor is aware of your teen's problems and can intervene quickly if he changes his mind.

In this week's L.E.A.P. plan, focus on the most challenging situation you have encountered in relation to your teen's medication. If he's not on medication and you would like to pursue this option, check with the doctor to see if this is indicated. If so, do a L.E.A.P. plan aimed at introducing the idea to your teen.

Key Points

- Have a routine for taking medication, so it is not forgotten.
- Make sure your child's doctor knows about any other medications he is on, including over-the-counter drugs and herbal treatments.
- Be patient. Medications take up to eight weeks at maximum tolerated dose to work, and appetite and sleep tend to improve before mood does.
- In the case of life-threatening side effects, go to the emergency department. If it's not life threatening but troublesome, ask your child's doctor for advice.

Remember:
1. Level of life stress and growth can affect medication requirements.
2. By combining CBT and medication, dosage can often eventually be lowered and the risk of relapse is decreased.
3. Long-term outcome of SSRIs is unknown, but so far so good.

In getting my child or teen to take medication, it would be helpful to:
1. Take at the same place at the same time every day (example: put beside juice on the dinner table).

2. _____

_____

_____

3. _____

_____

_____

4. _____

_____

_____

Your L.E.A.P. plan response for this week is:

The situation: _____

_____

_____

_____

Label your thoughts and feelings: _____

_____

_____

_____

Empathize with your teen: _____

_____

_____

_____

Explore ways to respond: _____

_____

_____

_____

Apply alternative idea/plan: _____

_____

_____

_____

Pick a follow-up time and plan ahead: _____

_____

_____

_____

Dealing with
the School

Depressed children often struggle at school. They struggle academically because of poor concentration and learned helplessness (the idea "I can't do it, so why bother"). They may have difficulty attending school because of low energy, anxiety, or depressive withdrawal. Poor attendance in turn exacerbates academic problems.

Socially, the depressed youngster often feels out of place at school. Peers and teachers are perceived as unfriendly and critical, even if this is not true, due to cognitive distortions. Thus, take your child's report of what is happening at school with a grain of salt. Don't accuse her of lying—she really perceives the situation exactly as described. But obtain some information about what's happening from another source

Progress Check

How did your L.E.A.P. plan related to medication work out this past week? Anything you'd like to modify, or is it better to just persevere with it one more week? Remember, one or two L.E.A.P. plans at a time is our recommendation. More than two at a time may be too many. If you are already juggling two plans, and your teen is struggling at school, put one plan aside this week so you can concentrate on school issues.

before storming into the principal's office to demand changes. In addition, depressed children's sullen behavior or glum facial expressions often invite criticism or rejection. The depressed child then takes this as further evidence that others are uncaring or that she is unlikable. Many children also fear being stigmatized for being depressed, for school absenteeism, or for seeing a psychiatrist (if others find out about this). Fear of stigma sometimes results in further school avoidance.

Overcoming School Avoidance

School avoidance is not always obvious in depressed teens. Some teens frankly refuse to go to school, but others may claim to be sick to avoid school or claim that they need more time off school even when their mood improves. Still others may leave the house but not attend classes, or attend only some classes and skip others. Assume that your depressed teen will perceive school as a challenge, and may need some time to make the transition back to full-time school attendance. Talking about what difficulties she anticipates going back will allow for some joint troubleshooting and reduce the chances that she will secretly avoid school.

If you're still concerned or if your child has a history of school avoidance in the past, negotiate a way to monitor attendance in the first few weeks back, with decreased monitoring as attendance becomes more consistent. For example, many schools have students keep a notebook or assignment book to track work completion in various subjects. Asking to see this notebook regularly to determine whether workload needs to be modified (as it sometimes does with depression) provides an unintrusive check on attendance, since it is unlikely your child can complete work in a subject without attending at least some classes. If your teen is amenable to at least one teacher being involved, that teacher can also provide updates on work completion and attendance. Having one regular contact person at the school is often more helpful than dealing with large numbers of teachers, and is more respectful of your teen's need for confidentiality.

For school avoidance, there are several ways to help. These include:

- *Get your child to attend school as much as she is able to.* Attendance can't be forced on a depressed teen, only encouraged, unless you involve a truant officer or other authority figure. Such use of authority may undermine your relationship with your teen, however, which may make matters worse in the long run.
- *To encourage attendance, talk to your teen about going to school as a positive, though challenging activity.* Find out if she needs help getting up in time for school and getting books together in the morning, to get back into a routine. Ask if she needs a ride to school, or if she can arrange to go with a friend each morning. Getting your teen through the school door is often the biggest hurdle! Then, provide praise and positive reinforcement for every step toward full attendance. Initially, for example, you

may negotiate with your teen to attend for part of the day, with her weekly allowance contingent on attending that part.

- *Ignore academic success or failure in the first few months back at school,* as depression may interfere with the academics initially. Merely attending school shows effort, and that's a step forward for a helpless/hopeless teen.

- *If school absence has been prolonged (more than a couple of weeks), re-entry into school should be gradual, if possible—* starting with one class and gradually building up as your child tolerates it. Your child's psychologist or psychiatrist can provide documentation about the need for this. To increase motivation and hopefulness, keep a record of each class attended to demonstrate to your teen that she is progressing.

- *Keeping school routines at home (same waking up time, same work time, same recreation time, same bedtime) can also facilitate school return.* Just keeping the routine should be reinforced initially; productive work comes later. Video games, television, and other entertainments should not be permitted during school hours. This approach also prevents teens from becoming "too comfortable" in the home environment, and thus encourages school return.

Communicating with the School

Depression often interferes with teens' ability to perform at school. The school needs to be aware of the problem if they are going to help. If neither you nor your depressed teen speak up, the school will assume that decreased performance is due to laziness, defiance, or some other behavioral problem, and will treat her accordingly. To continue coping with school, your teen will need, at a minimum, some modified academic expectations during the time that she is most depressed. Discuss exactly how to do this with the teacher(s) or principal. Some options include: basing final grades on your teen's work during the months she is not depressed, attending a summer program to catch up on missed work, temporary attendance at a learning center or special class during depressed times (or afterwards to catch up), or dropping a course or two (if in high school) with the provision for taking it at a later time.

To communicate with the school effectively:

- *Develop a good relationship with at least one professional at the school.* (The principal, guidance counselor, school psychologist, or school social worker are some good options; so is the homeroom teacher in the primary grades).

- *Find out how flexible the school is willing to be in helping your child reintegrate.* In Canada, school personnel who don't understand what depression is can be referred to a recent resource guide for teachers, called "When Something is Wrong" produced by the Canadian Psychiatric Research Foundation (www.cprf.ca). It is brief but to the point, and should convince most teachers that the child has a legitimate mental health problem. In the United States, a good resource is: "Depression in Children—A Handout for Teachers" from the National Association of School Psychologists (www.nasponline.org). You may also wish to share with teachers some fact sheets about depression found on the website of the American Academy of Child and Adolescent Psychiatry at www.aacap.org; information from the Depression and Bipolar Support Alliance at www.dbsalliance.org might also be helpful.

- *Follow up on a regular basis regarding your child's progress at school.* Don't expect teachers to call you. Find out when *you* can reach *them* on a regular basis.
- *Express some empathy for the school personnels' concerns and keep your own feelings in check, and they will be more likely to listen to you (again, use the L.E.A.P. plan!).* Try to be nonjudgmental, and focus on solving the problem. For example: "Here's what I find helpful in getting Heather to focus. Could something similar happen in the classroom? Who could implement this? What has been helpful with other students in this situation?" In other words, be willing to consider different alternatives, depending on the school's resources, and try out something you *both* think is reasonable. Then, remember to follow up to reassess things.

Special Programs

Some children have preexisting learning disabilities, and school failure contributes to their feelings of depression. If school failure precedes depression, learning problems should be suspected at the time of the initial mental health assessment. In this case, the depressed teen should be referred for a learning evaluation either through the school or privately.

In the U.S., if you ask the school to evaluate your child for possible learning disabilities, the evaluation will be done free of charge to you. However, you will not have a say over who does the evaluation and when (generally, a team of professionals, including a psychologist, speech-language therapist, special education teacher, occupational therapist, etc., will be involved). In addition, if the school determines that your child does have a learning problem that is interfering with her ability to keep up with the regular curriculum, they will recommend that she begin receiving special education services. In other words, you will not really be able to control what the school does with the results. This may be all to the good if your child needs special education services (such as from a special education teacher or a speech-language therapist). It may be a problem, though, if there is the possibility that you and the school disagree as to whether your child has a learning disability.

If you pursue a private evaluation for your child, you will have to pay for it yourself, and comprehensive learning evaluations can run into the thousands of dollars. However, you will be able to choose the professional(s) who will test your child. You will be able to discuss the results of the evaluation with the professional without involving the school. If you decide to share the results with the school, you will likely have some say over what is and is not included in the written report. The school will then be required to consider the results of the private evaluation in determining whether your child qualifies for special education.

If your child is determined to qualify for special education, you and the school personnel will develop an individualized education program (IEP) for your child. This is a document that specifies, among other things:

1. what individualized learning goals your child needs (such as developing specific reading or math skills or increasing her reading comprehension from a seventh-grade to an eighth-grade level);
2. what special services (such as instruction from a special education teacher) she needs to help her achieve them; and
3. in what setting (regular classroom, resource room, etc.) she will receive these services.
4. It also specifies modifications to the regular curriculum she might need (such as extra time for taking tests, or reduced homework).

If you suspect a learning problem, it is preferable to have a learning evaluation *after* the depression has been treated, as depression can mask a child's true learning potential and thus invalidate the evaluation.

Some children who have no learning difficulties when not depressed must temporarily go into a special education program because depressive symptoms are interfering with academic performance. If this is the case for your teen, ask her psychologist or psychiatrist to write a letter supporting this option on a time-limited basis. Help your teen to see this change in a positive light. A time-limited program of academic assistance that allows her to earn time in the mainstream classes through work completion is an excellent option, if available. It gives her hope of a return to the mainstream at her own pace, and strengthens the link between personal effort and positive results (lost in the "learned helpless" state). Special programs are also preferable to home instruction, as they usually occur within a school setting, reducing dependence on the home environment and often easing the transition to a regular classroom. Such transitions are not always accomplished smoothly, however, as Mary's story, below, illustrates.

Mary and Reintegration into School: *Organizing a gradual transition from a special program back to the regular classroom, or from home to the school environment, is difficult for some school personnel. Mary, a depressed girl of twelve, was making excellent progress in a special, small-class program with modified academic expectations. She felt ready to take the next step and start attending one or two regular classes. Unfortunately, her school insisted that she complete every single piece* *of work from the regular class (which she had not attended in five months) before being allowed back there for even part of the day.*

Mary realized that the pace of the special class was much slower than the regular class, so achieving this goal would take almost a year. She became discouraged and began swearing at the teacher of the "dummy class." She had a significant relapse of her depression. After several futile attempts to negotiate with the school, Mary's parents decided to look for a school that was more flexible around the reintegration process. Fortunately, they were able to find one, but Mary missed an additional three months as a result of her relapse.

School switches are not always the answer, though. They represent a dramatic, often difficult change in the child's life. For this reason, switching schools should be seen as a last resort. If the transition to the regular classroom is rocky, consider hiring a private tutor for your child, if possible, especially during the first few months. The expense is well worth it in the long run for many teens recovering from depression. Encourage the tutor to work in small chunks to avoid overwhelming your teen, and to praise even the most minimal academic effort.

Tutoring without school attendance is not advisable in most cases, though. It may be necessary if a depressed teen is hospitalized, but should not continue much beyond the hospitalization. Schools sometimes encourage this option, however, as it reduces the school's challenges related to accommodating a student with special needs. Unfortunately, this option reduces depressed teens' motivation to return to school because they perceive home study as less threatening than facing the outside world (as they would if going to school). Thus, social withdrawal related to depression is often exacerbated, social skills may be lost, and the teen may become increasingly dependent on her particular tutor (as opposed to learning to deal with a variety of teachers). Successful school return becomes increasingly unlikely the longer home tutoring without school attendance continues.

School Changes

Some teens are convinced that they cannot show their face at the same school again. Some parents feel, as Mary's parents did, that they are getting nowhere with personnel at their child's school. Some schools don't offer the programs your child may need, and sometimes the IEP may require placement at a different school. Whatever the reason, a school switch must sometimes be considered. This should be given careful thought, however, as it represents a major change in your child's environment (children spend up to half their waking hours at school), and change is stressful. Usually the stress is less if the change can be deferred to the start of the next school year or at least the next school term. Try to balance the disruption associated with the change against how bearable or unbearable the present situation is. Also, be sure that the next school really will be better for your child. A fresh start can be great for some children, but a new environment does not always solve old problems.

Finally, remember that even a "lost" year at school is not the end of the world. Being a year behind your friends is not fun, but the difference between graduating at seventeen and graduating at eighteen or nineteen is minimal in the long run.

Social Stigma

Almost all children and teens who have been absent from school for more than a few days are concerned about what others will think when they return. As in the example of Tammy earlier in the book, help your child prepare a phrase or two that will keep the "nosy" questions to a minimum. "I've been sick, but now I'm back" is a good standard response. "I'd rather not talk about it" or "I'll tell you some other time" are good follow-ups for the friends who insist on specifics. Your child may have one or two close friends with whom she shares more, but leave this to her discretion. Reconnecting with peers may be easier via one or two buddies anyway.

Inform the teachers (or have your teen inform the teachers, if that's her preference) of the reason for her absence, but ask that your child or teen not be singled out for this. Depending on the school, meeting with a guidance counselor or school psychologist might ease the transition. In some schools, the guidance office can be accessed easily with no attendant stigma, but trust your child's judgment if she says this is not the case at her school.

Negotiating with School Personnel

Even though, in Mary's case, negotiation with the school proved futile, it is still worth examining how to go about this process. Many schools are willing to be more flexible, with the right approach. What is the right approach? No surprise: try a L.E.A.P. plan!

Label thoughts and feelings: I am really *frustrated* with the school's unwillingness to gradually reintegrate my child. She's not disruptive in class, and would only need a little extra help academically. We've already said we'll pay for a tutor after class. What else do they want?

Empathize with the teacher (rather than your teen, in this case): Insisting that it's my right as a parent to have my child educated hasn't worked. The teacher just digs in her heels when I do that. The teacher does have thirty other children in her class, and even a few extra minutes with mine might be a strain. Also, she may remember some of my child's moodiness, difficult behavior, and suicidal statements that occurred before the depression was treated. She may be worried about dealing with that again. I also know the school board only pays for an educational assistant as long as the child is in a special program full time. Thus, allowing my child to gradually leave the special program may imply a loss of resources to the school.

Explore ways to respond: Maybe I need to talk to the next level of authority, like the IEP team, about having the educational assistant part-time. After all, there may be another child who could benefit from her help the rest of the time. This might take some of the pressure off the teacher and principal. If that doesn't work, maybe I can find someone to support my child in the classroom until she is completely comfortable, and reassure the teacher that this person will not disrupt her routine. Maybe a short meeting between my child and the teacher would be helpful, so she can see for herself how much better my daughter is now. She might also be more conciliatory in front of my daughter. They had a good relationship in the past.

Apply alternative idea/plan: I'll start with a short meeting with the teacher and my daughter, to explore the options I've thought about. I'll phone the special education supervisor as well, so I have some information on what the IEP team might be willing to do.

Pick a follow up time and plan ahead: After the meeting, I'll know if even a little modification on my child's behalf would be possible. Then, I'll follow up weekly to make sure it's implemented. If we get nowhere in the meeting, maybe I'll get back to the IEP team about other possible options. I'll also be sure to tell my child how proud I am of her participation in the process.

Exercise: Solving School-related Problems

How is your teen coping at school? Are there problems with her attendance? With academic catching-up? With social problems or stigmatization? With communication with school personnel?

Focus on the issue most relevant to your teen's situation, and make a L.E.A.P. plan for her main school-related difficulty this week. This difficulty could relate to attendance, to communicating with the school, to academic difficulties, or to challenges with social reintegration into school. Especially if you think your child needs to be in a special program, you may need to follow up with this over many weeks. Setting the wheels in motion for obtaining such a program can take patience and perseverance.

Key Points

- Encourage attendance and keep school routines, even at home.
- Negotiate gradual reintegration if your child's absence has been prolonged.
- Take an empathic, problem-solving approach with school personnel.
- Follow up regularly with your main school contact.
- Positively reinforce your teen's attendance and work completion separately.
- Consider a tutor if you are dissatisfied with academic help your child receives at school.
- Rehearse a phrase or two that helps your child deal with nosy questions.
- Inform the teacher and ask him or her not to single out your child by referring to her recent absence in front of peers.
- Allow your child to decide which peers know what.

Your L.E.A.P. plan response for this week is:

The situation: _____

_____

_____

_____

_____

Label your thoughts and feelings: _____

_____

_____

_____

_____

Empathize with your teen: _____

_____

_____

_____

_____

Explore ways to respond: _____

_____

_____

_____

_____

Apply alternative idea/plan: _____

_____

_____

_____

_____

Pick a follow-up time and plan ahead: _____

_____

_____

_____

_____

Dealing with Peers

For children and teens, peers can be wonderful and peers can be awful. They can be wonderful in supporting your child emotionally, and making him feel understood better than any grown-up possibly could. After all, they're in the same boat. They deal with the same joys and challenges as your child does and can give him a reassuring sense of belonging. Peer feedback can also provide invaluable information in the course of adolescent development. Peer reactions help teens realize how they affect others, and often prompt dramatic changes in behavior. In groups, peer influence is often profound—which is one reason we often use group therapy at this age.

Peers can be awful when the teen feels judged by them. Part of this perception of being judged all the time is normal in adolescence. Do you remember how hollow

Progress Check

How is your child or teen progressing at school? Did any ideas from last week help? Also, remember that we are almost at the end of the book, so if you want to work on an additional L.E.A.P. plan, there's no time like the present. Set aside a regular time each week (ten minutes should do) to keep reviewing progress after you finish the book. The work of thoughtful parenting goes on much longer than any book!

your parents' words sounded when they said, "Nobody will even notice that tiny zit on your face"? This feeling of being critically or judgmentally viewed by others is exacerbated by depressive thinking. Sometimes, there is also a realistic element to it. Cliques in middle school can be particularly cruel. Parents may also think peers are awful because they fear peers exerting a "bad influence" on their children.

Depressed Teens' Perspective on Peers

The truth is, peers are neither universally wonderful nor universally awful. Most children and teens experience a rich variety of peer relationships in the course of growing up. Depressed children are inclined to see peers more negatively because of cognitive distortions and low self-confidence. ("How could anyone possibly like a loser like me?") Distortions include:

- *perceiving rejection* when peers interact in neutral or noncommittal ways ("He didn't look at me today. I know he hates me");
- *dismissing positive peer interactions* ("She only talks to me because she pities me"); or
- *all-or-nothing thinking* ("I'm not in the popular group. I must be a complete nerd"; "Nobody is my soul mate. Therefore, I don't have any good friends").

Behaving according to these distortions can further erode peer relationships. Sullen, frowning teens who go into social situations with a chip on their shoulder (anticipating rejection) are more likely to be rejected. Teens who fear social criticism, on the other hand, often slouch, sit at the periphery of a group, or do not express their wishes for fear of offending someone. They are apt to be considered uninteresting by peers. In short, cognitive distortions reduce social effectiveness and thus can become self-fulfilling.

Improving Peer Relationships

Anything you can do to assist your teen in overcoming the above thoughts and behaviors is bound to be helpful. A few suggestions are:

- *Encourage him to "walk tall," even if he doesn't feel like it.* Playing a more socially successful role can sometimes help teens make a nice transition to really becoming more socially successful.
- *Invite your own friends over so that you can model appropriate social "approach" behaviors.* For example, telephone friends to set up a mutually convenient time to meet or invite friends to share a meal or go out for a meal as a group.
- *If your teen describes peer situations negatively, help him examine the evidence.* What really happened, and what did he infer (perhaps

incorrectly)? Is it possible that the other person deserves the benefit of the doubt until more evidence is found? Is there anything your child could do differently next time to affect the outcome?

- *Normalize some of the negative realities of middle school society* (for example, cliques that exclude other teens are very common at this age, particularly among girls), and encourage your child to "hang in there." Indicate that peer cruelty is not his fault, but rather due to the immaturity of the peers. Peer groups do become more inclusive and less judgmental as adolescents mature, and the "nerds" of middle school are often admired for their ability to help with assignments by the final grades of high school.

- *If your child has a few friends, help him value them.* Point out some of the nice times he has shared with the friends, even if they aren't part of the most popular group. Maybe the friends are not soul mates either, but that's OK. Some friends are just fun to go out with, even if you never tell them anything really serious.

- *If your teen has no friends but wants to make some, role-play conversation starters.* Any common sensory experience will do (sight, smell, sound, taste, touch). For example, "I wonder what planet they grew these potatoes on" might be a nice conversation starter in the school cafeteria, or, "I can't get that song by X (currently popular band) out of my head." Alternatively, have him ask a not-too-private question about the other person. People love to talk about themselves.

- *If your teen has even one friend, ask him if his buddy has other friends and would be willing to introduce him to them.* Perhaps your child can suggest a group activity to his buddy.

- *Peer activities can also lead to friendships, but to avoid disappointment, stress the fun of the activity* rather than telling him, "This is your chance to make friends." Encourage after-school activities that involve peers and might be interesting to your child.

- *If your child claims that nobody at his school has similar interests or might be a suitable friend, challenge this statement.* It's an example of extreme "all or nothing" thinking. Even if nobody is a perfect match, there are almost certainly some peers who are relatively compatible. Encourage approaching one of these relatively compatible peers, provided they are not known for aggression or ridiculing others. Sometimes, there is a group of peers that your child describes as boring. Discuss the possibility of joining that group, gaining acceptance, and gradually getting the group to do an activity your child might find less boring. It takes some patience, but changing the system from within is an option too few teens explore.

- *Encourage your child to reconnect with any old friends with whom he has lost touch since becoming depressed.* He may assume that these friends want nothing to do with him since he stopped calling them or acted "boring" around them due to depression. In reality, teenagers' memories are usually short, and unless there was a major disagreement that ended the friendship, most are quite happy to reconnect with old chums. If he fears a telephone call will be awkward, suggest he e-mail his old friends, as this may feel less threatening.

- *If your teen has a long-term pattern of social isolation that preceded and possibly contributed to his depression, ask his psychologist or psychiatrist to determine whether social phobia (also known as social anxiety) or another psychological disorder might be present.* (Social phobia is an anxiety disorder that makes people extremely sensitive to social embarrassment.) It may be that your child is just naturally shy—a variant of normal personality—but if another disorder is present, it will be important to treat that disorder to prevent your teen from becoming depressed again and to improve his social functioning. Social skills training and specific desensitization exercises are often helpful to teens with social phobia, and the psychologist or psychiatrist may be able to provide these or refer to a colleague who does. The psychologist or psychiatrist should also be able to determine whether the long-term social isolation is part of Asperger's syndrome, a developmental problem related to autism, and refer your child for appropriate treatment if this is present.

Bullies

All teens can be victimized by bullies, but depressed teens often appear isolated or unassertive, making them particularly easy targets. Bullying may also be a contributing factor to some teens' depression.

Bullies may need some additional intervention. Physical violence must be stopped, even if it means breaking your teen's confidence to ensure his safety. At a minimum, talk to the people in charge to obtain additional supervision of the playground, lunchroom, locker room, hallways, or other places where students are not usually under an adult's watchful eye. In more serious cases, discuss consequences for the perpetrator(s). Ideally, your child should report bullying of himself or others, and the school should respond sympathetically, with anti-bullying interventions. This rarely happens. Assuming it doesn't, you can still talk to your child about:

- *Reporting bullying, regardless of who is the victim, to protect everyone from further attack.* Inevitably, this will be considered "snitching" or "tattling," but remind your child that snitching is designed to get someone in trouble; reporting a bully is designed to keep someone safe. Usually, bullying is reported to the nearest teacher, but some schools have designated individuals to whom to report bullying incidents. Also, while many schools have a "zero tolerance" policy for physical violence, there may not be clear guidelines regarding taunting or verbal threats. Encourage your child to err on the side of caution, and report any incidents where someone might be at risk of harm.

- *Reducing the risk of being a victim.* Some things to do include:
    - Walking with your head held high;
    - Not crying or yelling or hitting in response to teasing (it inadvertently rewards the teaser with attention);
    - Using assertive statements when teased (for example, "That's not true. It's just your opinion");
    - Observing how peers handle teasing effectively;
    - Spending time with friends (isolated kids are easier to victimize than groups);
    - Avoiding unsupervised areas of the school or the school yard.

Teasing or ostracism are milder forms of bullying. If it's mutual (that is, your child is sometimes teased but sometimes the teaser), see if the teens can resolve it themselves. If your child is frequently the victim, resist the temptation to say, "Just ignore it." That's about as easy to do as ignoring an abscessed tooth. Instead, ask about assertive responses that your child has seen other peers use and encourage these. Then, in addition, help him come up with some reassuring self-talk for teasing situations. For example, he can say to himself: "Everyone has something different about them, mine just happens to be X"; "One hundred years from now, nobody will remember my bad complexion/ clothes/figure, etc., but the good things I did may still have an impact"; "In country X, I'd fit right in"; "People who need to tease to feel good about themselves must be pretty insecure"; or "Not everyone thinks that way; I know person X, person Y, and person Z don't").

Refer to Barbara Coloroso's book, *The Bully, the Bullied, and the Bystander.* There are also books designed for teens themselves, such as *Bullies are a Pain in the Brain* or *Being Bullied: You're Not Alone*, that may be useful to your teen (see Bibliography).

Peer Pressure

What about the peers who try to pressure your child into taking part in illicit activities? These characters can sometimes be a problem for depressed teens, who will do almost anything to gain peer approval. Online predators have become a particular menace recently.

In general, there is no substitute for good supervision in protecting children. Use whatever electronic and other devices are needed to block access to certain sites, chat rooms, TV channels, etc. and know what your children are exposed to in the media. Have rules for computer-based interactions and consequences for breaking them. For example, no child should meet someone for the first time based solely on contact via a chatline. Similarly, your teen should not disclose personal information online that might allow recognition or unwelcome contact (for example, address, phone number). Remind your teen that anyone he meets online is a stranger, and warrants the same caution as a stranger on the street. That doesn't mean teens should fear going online, but they should follow certain basic safety rules.

At the same time, recognize that there are limits. You can only monitor closely what happens under your own roof. Rather than sending spies to follow your teen, focus on good communication. Express interest in knowing who his friends are. Find out what the friends like to do together. Indicate that you know what goes on in the world (illegal drugs, for example, existed in most high schools even when we were young), without immediately expressing a disapproving opinion. (For example, don't say, "If I ever caught you doing that, I would ground you for life!"). Instead, listen and paraphrase what your teen is saying to make sure you've understood, and to indicate that the subject is open for discussion. Open lines of communication promote healthy relationships, and healthy relationships with parents, peers, and dating partners are prerequisites to healthy social behaviors in teens.

If you worry that your child may be tempted to cope with stress in unhealthy ways, offer a healthy alternative. Model how you cope with stress, and practice what you preach. For example, take a walk with your teen when you are both stressed, put on a yoga video, or listen to some relaxing music. Demonstrate a positive alternative rather than lecturing on the evils of drugs and drink.

If you have evidence that your child is engaging in illicit activities, set a limit and have a consequence for any further infractions. If there is potential danger involved, you are justified in looking for evidence of infractions regardless of privacy concerns, but try to reduce the intrusions on your teen's space after a few weeks of good behavior. Explain that your trust has to be earned, but when it is, you will be quite happy to "back off." If you have no evidence, go back to close supervision, good communication, and positive modeling. Unfounded accusations undermine trust, and therefore drive whatever is going on further underground. Also, your child is much more likely to resist peer pressure if he has a close, trusting relationship with you. Recall the example of Marcy:

Marcy (reviewed): *Marcy's depression was associated with very difficult behavior. Unlike some depressed teens, Marcy was hardly ever in her room. She began staying out later and later, then slept in until noon the next day. She met a new "boyfriend" online, and began to meet him at shopping malls. He was much older than she was, and had an extensive police record. She stopped calling her former friends from the debating team and the school band, and found a new crowd at school. Her new friends skipped class and experimented with various drugs. When her mother pointed out the risks of her behavior, Marcy just shrugged her shoulders. "So what? I don't deserve any better."*

Because Marcy had an aunt who had bipolar disorder, she was initially assessed for this diagnosis. She did not have most of the features of this disorder, though, and a careful history revealed that not all of her behavior problems started with the depression. She had always been rather disrespectful toward her parents, frequently swearing at them, and did not do any chores at home. She was bright, though, and her academically oriented friends had helped her stay involved in several school activities. As long as she had kept this particular group of friends, everything appeared fine on the surface.

Marcy's situation illustrates how a teen's lack of closeness to her parents can result in undue dependence on his peer group. Initially, Marcy's strong allegiance to her peers had a positive effect. Her peer group promoted studiousness and socially acceptable behavior. When the peer group changed to a more antisocial one, however, the result was disastrous. You've already heard in a previous chapter about a L.E.A.P. plan Marcy's mother developed for repeated curfew violations. A second plan was required when her mother's worst fear came true, and she found her daughter was engaging in drug abuse.

Marcy's mother was cleaning out her room when she came upon a small package behind her bed. She was shocked to learn that it was marijuana. She became furious at the thought that, in addition to her other misbehaviors, Marcy was now smoking drugs. Marcy's mother came up with this L.E.A.P. plan:

Label thoughts and feelings: I want to scream at that girl! After everything we've been through, now she does this! No matter what I do, she doesn't change her ways! What if she gets addicted? What is she doing to get the money for drugs? I feel like a total *failure* as a mother.

Empathize with your teen: I know screaming at her won't help. Maybe she hopes the drugs will make her depression go away. Maybe she feels pressured to smoke them because her new friends do. Maybe she even wanted me to find the drugs, to show her dad and me how bad her life has become. Maybe it's her way of showing she needs help.

Explore ways to respond: First, I need her dad to join me in managing this so we're both on the same page. We need to agree on an approach that indicates we're taking it seriously, but want to hear her side of the story as well. Then, maybe we could find a time to sit down with her when we're all calm. We could share the improvements in Marcy's behavior we've already noticed, and her great potential for the future. Maybe her dad could tell Marcy that I found the drugs, and that we were both disappointed (rather than furious) at the discovery. We need to give her a chance to explain herself, and be supportive of her as a person, but firmly explain why we cannot condone her drug-taking behavior.

As a consequence, we could ground her from going out with her friends this weekend, but still allow her telephone contact. We should also encourage her to tell her doctor about this. Who knows what the drugs could do in combination with her antidepressants! If she is open to that idea, we could encourage a discussion with a youth addiction counselor as well. Most importantly, we need to remain calm and matter-of-fact, so nobody loses their cool. If she sees we're intervening to help her, rather than punish or blame her, she's less likely to storm off. In the long run, she might even appreciate that her parents are not willing to give up on her.

Apply alternative ideas/plan: Marcy's mother acted on the ideas she had explored. Her husband was surprisingly supportive, now that they were dealing with a "serious" problem, rather than just an issue with curfews. Marcy agreed to tell her doctor, grudgingly accepted the grounding, but refused the addiction counseling and was hurt that anyone would think she was an "addict." Her parents were satisfied with the result, provided she agreed to a weekly room-check.

Pick a follow up time and plan ahead: Marcy's parents agreed to meet with her weekly for a month, not only to check her room but to follow up on how the plan was going and whether or not weekend privileges were in order. They also decided to speak to an addictions expert themselves, to get more advice about how to handle their daughter's difficulty.

Despite everything you've read, we're not saying that strong peer bonds are necessarily bad. As described earlier, peers can be wonderful in many ways. There needs to be a balance, however, in the relative strength of peer relationships and home relationships. Too much emphasis on either at the expense of the other can spell trouble. Recall Amanda, for example, who had no strong peer bonds. She could have received great benefit from a friend's perspective on her family. Marcy and Amanda represent two unhealthy extremes. Healthy teens feel connected to both their families and their peers, and they learn different things about themselves in the context of each of these interpersonal bonds.

Exercise: Promoting Healthy Peer Influences

What do you think of your child's or teen's peers? Do you feel that he needs to socialize more? What have you tried to be helpful? Do you fear that he may be exposed to negative peer influences? How are you dealing with this? Develop a L.E.A.P. plan for the peer-related problem most relevant to your child or teen. Remember, however, that you can't force friends upon your teen or force others to like him. Your teen will have to make an effort to make himself likeable and to like others in return. You can perhaps nudge him towards situations where friendships are possible, but he needs to do the work of making friends himself.

Key Points

- Help your teen correct negative or all-or-nothing thinking about peers by examining the evidence.
- Encourage him to "walk tall" and give others the benefit of the doubt.
- Try peer-based activities, conversation starters, or "buddies" if your child has too few friends.
- Provide close supervision, good communication, and positive modeling if your child has the wrong kind of friends, and don't make accusations unless you have proof.
- Remind the victim of peer teasing or ostracism that it is due to peer immaturity (i.e., not your child's fault) and does get gradually better as others grow up.
- Encourage both assertive behavior and reassuring self-talk if your teen is frequently teased
- Never tolerate bullying, and encourage your child not to tolerate it either, regardless of who is the victim

Your L.E.A.P. plan response for this week is:

The situation: _____
_____
_____
_____
_____

Label your thoughts and feelings: _____
_____
_____
_____
_____

Empathize with your teen: _____
_____
_____
_____
_____

Explore ways to respond: _____
_____
_____
_____
_____

Apply alternative idea/plan: _____
_____
_____
_____
_____

Pick a follow-up time and plan ahead: _____
_____
_____
_____
_____

The Future

As we approach the end of the book, take the opportunity to review any L.E.A.P. plans you have put into practice. One or two may stand out as "winners," while others may need some adjustments, or may not be worth pursuing. Decide what changes you will continue to work on, and find that ten or fifteen minutes a week to follow up. Also, keep records of everything you've tried, successfully or not, in a safe place. Some things may not work this month or even this year, but would be worth another try later.

This is the last chapter. At this point, many parents ask, with some trepidation, "What does my child's future hold?" None of us can gaze in the crystal ball and tell you for certain what will happen, but we can examine the possibilities, and how to improve the odds of your child or teen coping well longer term.

Single Episode or Chronic Problem?

People who have depression once are vulnerable to getting it again, and the stress needed to trigger it tends to be less the next time (termed the "kindling effect"). That is why early intervention and return to normal development and normal function is so important. Thus, by coming for treatment early in the course of your teen's illness, you have already taken the most important step.

A single episode of depression doesn't need to be the end of the world. Many teens recover and go on to lead happy, productive lives. Some, unfortunately, go on to further episodes or to other mental health problems. The treatments we have are certainly effective for resolving depressed mood in the short term, but this does not necessarily mean that it won't come back. Recurrence is common, and recurrent depression often needs longer-term treatment. This can include "booster sessions" of additional psychotherapy or longer-term medication treatment.

> **Sharon and Adulthood:** *Sharon had an initial episode of depression in her teens, recovered, relapsed five years later after a serious car accident, recovered, and relapsed again five years after that when her first child was born (so-called "postpartum depression"). Each time she was depressed, she responded well to a combination of medication and brief psychotherapy. Between episodes, she is a highly respected professional in her field, and is very happily married. Nevertheless, we are now discussing longer-term medication, at least until she completes her family, as she is at very high risk (up to 90 percent chance) of a further relapse when she has more children.*

We are always pleasantly surprised, when we follow up some of the graduates of our program, to find some of them denying they ever had a problem. It complicates our research, of course, but speaks to the resilience of young people. On the other hand, for some teens depression will be an ongoing part of life. For these young people, the emphasis needs to be on what can be accomplished, learned, and enjoyed at times when they are not depressed. Like the young woman above, they can still have very satisfying lives.

Can Continued Mental Health Be Ensured?

Continued mental health cannot be guaranteed, because some factors are beyond your control. As teens become more independent, for example, they can make life choices that increase their risk for further depression. Teens with bipolar disorder, with depression that has psychotic features, with strong family histories of mood disorder, and with more than one episode of depression are also particularly vulnerable to relapse.

Nevertheless, going back to what you learned in this book can improve your child's odds. For example, you can't change children's genetic vulnerability, but you can change how you relate to them and to yourself. You can't prevent stress in the life of your child, but you can encourage her to use the tools needed to deal with it effectively. In addition, you can encourage regular physical exercise, a simple thing that has been proven to reduce the risk of relapse in depression.

It is also worthwhile to help your child recognize the signs that she may be getting depressed again. Then, you can encourage her to go back to the professional she talked to the last time she was depressed. Remember, intervening early often results in a shorter, less severe, and less debilitating episode of depression.

What If There Is a Relapse of Depression?

If there is relapse, you can't take away the helplessness your child feels when becoming depressed. You can make sure she gets help early, and you can look for the strengths she has apart from the illness. You can't take away her negative moods, but you can show her how it's possible to cope in healthy ways. You can try to understand how you feel, how your child feels, and what attitudes or actions might make a positive difference. That's the L.E.A.P. plan in a nutshell, and it's designed to prevent *parents* from feeling helpless!

It is also important, when seeking help for your child or teen, to go back to whomever was helpful initially, if possible. Not only are you likely to be seen more quickly there than with someone new, but the trusting relationships that exist between you, the professional, and your adolescent are likely to facilitate recovery. If you do see a new professional, make sure it's clear who is responsible for your child's overall treatment plan (to avoid nobody having this role), and never see multiple professionals without advising each about the others' involvement. If you, your child, or your spouse are not sure whether or not depression is returning, it doesn't hurt to go back to the previous therapist to check out this possibility. When dealing with a possible relapse, it's "better safe than sorry."

Dana (continued): *Dana is the thirteen-year-old girl you met in Chapter 6 who was a very picky eater, and could never decide on a restaurant. This symptom was, however, part of a serious depressive episode. While she was recovering from her depression, Dana and her mother and sister had an unfortunate experience resulting from a restaurant visit: they got food poisoning. Dana was hospitalized and needed over a week to recover from the food poisoning. This incident triggered a relapse of her depression. As part of the relapse, she ate even less and complained of ongoing stomach pains.*

Unfortunately, rather than continuing psychotherapy and antidepressant treatment with Dana's doctor, her mother decided to stop all previous treatment. She got a referral for Dana to a gastroenterologist to further investigate the stomach pains. Dana's history of depression was not shared with this doctor, and the investigations continued. Dana's mother also decided to sue the restaurant for damages and got the gastroenterologist to testify on her behalf. The protracted lawsuit, ongoing medical investigations, sudden discontinuation of antidepressant treatment, and loss of her previous therapist all added stress to Dana's situation. A year later, she had recovered from her stomach pains and from the worst of her depressive symptoms, but remained socially isolated and unable to attend school.

Dana's story illustrates why it is important to try to address relapse with the same mental health professional who provided treatment originally, rather than pursuing a different course of treatment. Sometimes, what is triggering the relapse can be identified and nipped in the bud. Often, a few sessions to review previously learned coping skills can be helpful. Resuming medication (if it has been stopped) may be indicated. The professional may also be able to go over standardized measures of depression to evaluate the severity of the relapse and compare it to the last episode. Suicidal risk should also be reevaluated.

In Dana's case, ideally, her mother would have recognized the resumption of picky eating and stomach pains as part of the depression, after Dana was medically cleared by the doctors at the hospital. She then would have gone back to the original treating mental health professional and described Dana's reaction to the food poisoning. He or she would then have talked to Dana and reviewed the previous treatment plan. Together with Dana and her mother, this doctor could then have decided what parts of the treatment plan should continue (for example, antidepressant medication), and what should be added to deal with the stomach pains (for example, increasing activity and doing some relaxation exercises focused on abdominal muscles). By continuing with the same doctor, Dana could have avoided having to reestablish a trusting relationship with someone new and could have avoided the discomfort of further medical investigations. Most likely, this would have resulted in faster progress. Avoiding the court proceedings, if possible, would have been advisable. Court proceedings almost always prolong the recovery process, as these proceedings inadvertently give teens reasons to maintain their symptoms.

How Are You and Your Teen Doing Now?

It may be that your teen has improved considerably as you've progressed through this book and worked with one or more professionals. On the other hand, it may seem as if she's no further ahead or even doing worse. In part, this depends on how quickly you proceeded through the book. Even well-treated depressive episodes can take several months to improve, depending on your teen's response to psychotherapy and/or antidepressant medication.

If it's been several months, however, and things appear to be going downhill, ask to meet with your teen's psychologist or psychiatrist. He or she may have a better idea of why your teen appears "stuck." For example, teens sometimes share stressful events with their therapists that their parents may not be aware of. Alternately, the professional may be just as puzzled as you are. In this case, it may be helpful to review what parts of the treatment plan are working and what parts may need modification. For example: Is your teen really taking her antidepressants each day? Is there an ongoing problem at school that is preventing her from feeling better? Are there family problems that require additional counseling? Could your teen be abusing alcohol or another substance that is interfering with recovery from depression? Explore these possibilities, and negotiate some reasonable modifications with the professional and your teen.

One other possibility is that your teen really is doing better, but the change has been so gradual that you have had difficulty noticing it. Go over the symptoms of depression described at the beginning of this book (page 11)and rate them again on a scale from 1 to 4, without looking at your first set of ratings. Are your ratings now even slightly better than at the beginning? Waiting for change in depressed teens can be like watching grass grow: it's too slow to notice day by day, but there is a difference over several weeks.

If your teen seems even a little bit better, that's great! Keep doing what you're doing and look for more progress in the weeks to come. If you find yourself feeling discouraged despite her progress, take a moment to reflect on your own state of mind. Are you being overly pessimistic yourself? Are you experiencing some of the cognitive distortions described in Chapter 9? If so, consider seeing a professional yourself to assess the possibility of depression. As we've said at several points in this book, depression does run in families. Remember, if you may be depressed yourself, working to improve your own mental health may be one of the greatest gifts you can give your teen.

A Final Word

No matter how clever we think we are, a certain amount of improvement in depressed teens depends on the adolescent herself in the long run. We often think of ourselves as helping depressed teens, but if we are honest, we must admit that we only help them help themselves. Realizing this, we have one final suggestion: try expecting more of your depressed child or teen than she expects of herself. It can help. For example, in a classic psychology experiment, teachers were told certain pupils in their class had scored exceptionally well on a test at the beginning of the year. The students' names were chosen at random, and none were really exceptionally bright. Nevertheless, by the end of the year, the students the teachers had expected to do well were at the top of their classes. Believing in people's potential does make a difference.

Finally, give yourself and your child or teen credit for fighting depression and for persevering with this program. Positively reinforce "the right stuff" whenever you see it in him or her, and in yourself.

Exercise: Thinking Long Term

How do you plan to follow up on the information you have learned about depression, your teen, and yourself in the course of reading this book and doing the suggested activities?

What are your thoughts and concerns about the future for your child or teen?

What problems are you still facing with your adolescent? If needed, make one final L.E.A.P. plan for what you see as the biggest problem still facing her.

Key Points

- Find a safe place to store the written material (i.e., L.E.A.P. plans) you developed while working through this book.
- Find ten minutes in next week's schedule to review what you are doing to help your child with depression.
- Give yourself and your child or teen a positive reward for persevering with this program.
- Believe in your depressed child or teen, to help him or her L.E.A.P. ahead!

My long-term L.E.A.P. response(s) is/are:
(list the 'keepers')

The situation: _____

_____

_____

_____

_____

Label your thoughts and feelings: _____

_____

_____

_____

_____

Empathize with your teen: _____

_____

_____

_____

_____

Explore ways to respond: _____

_____

_____

_____

_____

Apply alternative idea/plan: _____

_____

_____

_____

_____

Pick a follow-up time and plan ahead: _____

_____

_____

_____

_____

My long-term L.E.A.P. response(s) is/are:
(list the 'keepers')

The situation: _____

_____

_____

_____

Label your thoughts and feelings: _____

_____

_____

_____

Empathize with your teen: _____

_____

_____

_____

Explore ways to respond: _____

_____

_____

_____

Apply alternative idea/plan: _____

_____

_____

_____

Pick a follow-up time and plan ahead: _____

_____

_____

_____

My long-term L.E.A.P. response(s) is/are:
(list the 'keepers')

The situation: _____

_____

_____

_____

_____

Label your thoughts and feelings: _____

_____

_____

_____

_____

Empathize with your teen: _____

_____

_____

_____

_____

Explore ways to respond: _____

_____

_____

_____

_____

Apply alternative idea/plan: _____

_____

_____

_____

_____

Pick a follow-up time and plan ahead: _____

_____

_____

_____

_____

My long-term L.E.A.P. response(s) is/are:
(list the 'keepers')

The situation: _____

_____

_____

_____

_____

Label your thoughts and feelings: _____

_____

_____

_____

_____

Empathize with your teen: _____

_____

_____

_____

_____

Explore ways to respond: _____

_____

_____

_____

_____

Apply alternative idea/plan: _____

_____

_____

_____

_____

Pick a follow-up time and plan ahead: _____

_____

_____

_____

_____

Bibliography

American Academy of Child and Adolescent Psychiatry. "Facts for Families." www.aacap.org.

American Psychiatric Association (1994). *Diagnostic and Statistical Manual of Mental Disorders, Fourth Edition (DSM-IV)*. Washington, DC: American Psychiatric Association.

Bay, E. *The Serenity Audiotape* and *The Relaxation Route Audiotape*. Toronto, Ontario, Canada: Relaxation Response Institute, 2000. (www.elibay.com)

Bay, E. *Relaxation CD Series (Let Go; Going Deep; Mind-body Software and Sleep)*. Toronto, Ontario: Relaxation Response Institute, 2003. (www.elibay.com)

Beck, A., Ward, C.H., Mendelson, M., Mock, J., and Erbaugh, J. (1961). "An inventory for measuring depression." *Archives of General Psychiatry*. Jun;4 : 561-71.

Burns, D. *Feeling Good Handbook*. New York, NY: Plume, 1999.

Canadian Psychiatric Research Foundation. *When Something's Wrong: Ideas for Teachers with Troubled Students*. Toronto, Ontario: CPRF, 2002. (www.cprf.ca)

Coloroso, B. *The Bully, The Bullied, and the Bystander.* New York, NY: Harper Collins, 2002.

Fassler, D.G. and Dumas, L.S. *Help Me, I'm Sad.* New York, NY: Penguin Books, 1997.

Greene, R. W. *The Explosive Child: A New Approach for Understanding and Helping Easily Frustrated, "Chronically Inflexible" Children.* 2nd ed. New York, NY: Harper Collins, 2001.

Kaufman, M. *Helping Your Teen Overcome Depression: A Guide for Parents.* Toronto, Ontario: Key Porter Books, 2000.

Kelbaugh, G. *Can I Catch It Like a Cold?* Toronto, Ontario: Centre for Addiction and Mental Health Publications, 2002.

Kovacs, M. et al. (1997). "A Controlled Family History of Study of Childhood Onset Depressive Disorder." *Archives of General Psychiatry.* 54 (7), 613-623.

Manassis, K.M. *Keys to Parenting Your Anxious Child.* Hauppauge, NY: Barron's Educational Series, Inc., 1996.

National Association of School Psychologists. "Depression in Children—A Handout for Teachers." www.nasp.org.

Nicholson, J., Henry, A., Clayfield, J., and Phillips, S. *Parenting Well When You Are Depressed: A Complete Resource for Maintaining a Healthy Family.* Oakland, CA: New Harbinger Publications, 2001.

Oster, G.D. and Montgomery, S.S. *Helping Your Depressed Teenager: A Guide for Parents and Caregivers.* New York, NY: John Wiley and Sons, 1995.

Phelan, T. *Surviving Your Adolescents: How to Manage and Let Go of Your 13 to 18 Year Olds.* 2nd ed. Glen Ellyn, IL: Child Management, 1998.

Reivich, K. & Shatte, A. *The Resilience Factor.* New York, NY: Broadway Books, 2002.

Romain, T. *Bullies Are a Pain in the Brain.* Minneapolis, MN: Free Spirit Publishing, 1997. (www.freespirit.com)

Soloman, J.M. (2002). *Being Bullied: You're Not Alone.*

Tomm, K. "Towards a Cybernetic Systems Approach to Family Therapy at the University of Calgary." In D. S. Freeman (Ed.), *Perspectives on Family Therapy* (pp. 3-18). Vancouver, British Columbia: Butterworth & Co., 1980.

Resources

American Academy of Child & Adolescent Psychiatry
3615 Wisconsin Ave., NW,
Washington, DC 20016-3007
202-966-7300; 202-966-2891 (fax)
www.aacap.org

American Medical Association
515 N. State St.
Chicago, IL 60610
800-621-8335
www.ama-assn.org

American Psychological Association
750 First Street, NE,
Washington, DC 20002-4242
800-374-2721; 202-336-5510
www.apa.org

Canadian Academy of Child & Adolescent Psychiatry
Canadian Psychiatric Association
260-441 MacLaren Street

Ottawa, Ontario K2P 2H3
613-234-2815; 613-234-9857 (fax)

Canadian Medical Directory
Service in English: 416-442-2010 or 800-408-9431
Service in French: 514-630-5955 or 800-363-1327
www.mdselect.com

Toronto Office	*Montreal Office*
1450 Don Mills Road	1 Holiday Street - East Tower, Suite 705
Don Mills, Ontario	Pointe Claire, Quebec
M3B 2X7	H9R 5N3

Canadian Mental Health Association
8 King Street East, Suite 810
Toronto ON M5C 1B5
416-484-7750; 416-484-4617 (fax)
www.cmha.ca

Depression and Bipolar Support Alliance (DBSA)
730 N. Franklin Street, Suite 501
Chicago, IL 60610-7224
800-826-3632; 312-642-7243 (fax)
www.dbsalliance.org

The Mood Disorders Association of Ontario
40 Orchard View Blvd., Suite 222
Toronto, Ontario M4R 1B9
416-486-8046; 888-486-8236; 416-486-8127 (fax)
www.mooddisorders.on.ca

The Mood Disorders Society of Canada
Suite 763, 3-304 Stone Road West
Guelph, On, N1G 4W4
519-824-5565; 519-824-9569 (fax)
www.mooddisorderscanada.ca

National Alliance for the Mentally Ill (NAMI)
Colonial Place Three
2107 Wilson Blvd., Suite 300
Arlington, VA 22201
800-950-NAMI (6262)
888-344-6264 (TDD)
www.nami.org

National Association of School Psychologists
4340 East West Highway, Suite 402
Bethesda, MD 20814
301-657-0270; 301-657-0275 (fax)
www.nasp.org

National Institute of Mental Health
Office of Communications
6001 Executive Blvd., Room 8184, MSC 9663
Bethesda, MD 20892-9663
866-615-6464 (toll-free); 301-443-2379 (fax)
301-443-8431 (TDD)
www.nimh.nih.gov

Ontario Psychological Association
730 Yong St., Suite 221
Toronto, Ontario M4Y 2B7
416-961-5552; 800-268-0069 (referrals)
www.psych.on.ca

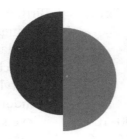

Index

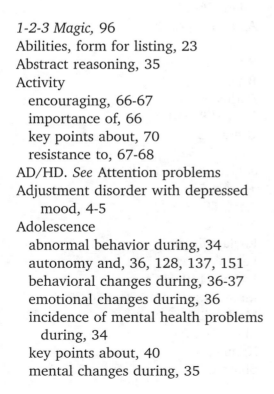

About the Authors

Katharina Manassis, MD, FRCPC

Katharina Manassis has graduate degrees in medicine and psychiatry. She works at the Hospital for Sick Children in Toronto, Ontario, where she founded and continues to lead the Anxiety Disorders Program. In addition, she is Associate Professor in the Department of Psychiatry at the University of Toronto, a researcher of childhood anxiety disorders, and author of professional papers, plus a book, **KEYS TO PARENTING YOUR ANXIOUS CHILD** (Barrons Educational Series, 1996). Dr. Manassis lives with her family in Pickering, Ontario.

Anne Marie Levac, RN, MN

Anne Marie Levac is an Advanced Practice Nurse in the Child, Youth and Family Program at the Centre for Addiction and Mental Health in Toronto, Ontario. She holds a Master's in Nursing from the University of Calgary where she specialized in family systems nursing. She is a Lecturer in the Faculty of Nursing and the Department of Psychiatry at the University of Toronto. She specializes in child, marriage, and family therapy for children and families experiencing psychosocial problems. She lives with her husband in Oakville, Ontario.